Black Mental Health Matters

The Ultimate Guide for Mental Health Awareness in the Black Community

Aaren Snyder, LMFT

Library of Congress Control Number: 2020904653
ISBN: 9780578651897

Printed by Ingram Content Group, in the United States of America.

Majestic Publishing
2042 Southmoor Dr.
Toledo, OH 43609

www.thementalhealthmatters.com

Contents

*"If there's a book you really want to read
but it hasn't been written yet,
then you must write it.*

–Toni Morrison"

Preface

I wrote this book to serve as a method of increasing mental health awareness in neglected communities—especially the *black community*. Throughout the near-decade I've spent as a mental health practitioner, I've noticed that a lack of awareness and understanding of mental health issues has in many cases, perpetuated many of the problems that plague our community. So, I decided to utilize the training, experience, and general knowledge I've accumulated by working in the mental health field to provide a thorough, easy to understand explanation of various esoteric concepts, theories, and facts that are typically limited to those working within the mental health field.

Also, I will dispel some of the negative beliefs that surround mental health. Throughout this book, I use the terms African-American/black and brown community, lower socioeconomic status community, and impoverished communities interchangeably. However, I am by no means insinuating that all black/brown communities are of lower socioeconomic status or impoverished; nor am I implying that this book's content *only* applies to black and brown people or other marginalized groups.

The intention of the information in *Black Mental Health Matters* is not to replace adequate treatment from a professional or to be used as a comprehensive guide for understanding mental health issues. Its purpose is to educate those who are uneducated about mental health and to enhance the knowledge of those who wish to learn more about psychological issues that are significant aspects of their lives. Overall, *Black Mental Health Matters* aims to enhance mental health awareness and literacy in black and brown communities, as well as in other underprivileged societies.

Introduction

I have spent several years working in the mental health field. My journey as a mental health practitioner began in 2007 as a student at Central State University in Wilberforce, Ohio. There, I earned a bachelor's degree in Psychology.

Shortly after, I landed my first job in the mental health field as a hotline worker in the psych unit of a hospital in northeast Ohio. This job made me second-guess working in mental health. There was never a dull moment in the psych unit. I spoke with individuals who were dealing with all kinds of problems, ranging from relationship troubles or problems at work to crisis situations like severe suicidal ideation.

Many, if not all, of the patients I spoke with were living with mental illnesses, some of which had been detected, diagnosed, and treated by a licensed mental health professional (MHP). Yet, many of the patients I spoke to were dealing with psychological issues that flew under the radar. Both the treated and untreated clients had similar symptoms, but the patients who called in to the hotline with untreated problems usually displayed amplified versions of their symptoms.

Patients who were untreated typically called in with more severe and complex problems. They also had minimal insight into their issues, making it more difficult for me to resolve the situations they needed help with. Typically, these clients were referred to me after experiencing suicidal ideation. The patients who had received prior treatment had more of an understanding of their situations and used practical coping strategies, along with the services I provided. My experiences in the psych unit demonstrated how much of a difference getting (or not getting) mental help at the right time could make in a person's life.

After finishing a two-year tenure at the hospital, I went on to work at a group home in northern Ohio as a direct care professional (DCP) and case manager for developmentally disabled (DD) and mentally ill children. The children at the group home were between the ages of 7 and 18. All of the children had severe psychological issues, which in most instances, were shaped by highly unfortunate circumstances (i.e., neglect, emotional, physical, verbal, and sexual abuse).

To say the group home residents had difficult personalities would be misleading. A more fitting statement is that they were a pain in my ass! To an untrained eye, their behavior would've been seen as inherent character flaws, or even worse—pure evil. But, their actions actually were the result of years of dysfunctional living situations, which led to the development of various maladaptive behaviors and ineffective coping skills.

After moving on from the group home, I went to work as a substance abuse and mental health case manager/screener at a county jail in northwest Ohio. While working at the jail, I began to recognize the connection between mental health and mass incarceration.

Though most of them were unaware, many of the inmates at the county jail were dealing with severe mental illnesses like depression, schizophrenia, bipolar disorder, and anxiety. A large number of the inmates had been raised—and were currently living in—circumstances not conducive to their emotional wellbeing. Many of the inmates experienced psychological trauma—poverty, substance abuse, molestation, neglect, and some had even witnessed severe violence or death.

Another observation that I made at the jail was that many police officers, correctional officers, and civilians who report perceived or actual criminal activity often do not recognize the signs of a mental health crisis. And for that reason, many psychological issues are treated in the same way as crimes. This lack of knowledge is especially problematic in judicial and correctional spheres and has led to unfair imprisonment of countless people, and in some cases—death.

While working at the jail, I obtained a Chemical Dependency Counselor Assistant license (CDCA). As a CDCA, I led substance abuse support groups. In our meetings, people talked about their abusive parents or spouses. They'd bring up being raped, or doing time in prison. Just about every messed up situation you can think of, I heard it at a group meeting.

At the groups, I noticed again an incredibly familiar pattern that I had also seen at the jail—and nearly everywhere I've worked in the mental health field. Most, if not all, of the group participants came from awful living conditions that did not encourage emotional wellness.

Soon after my time at the county jail ended, I received my master's degree in Marriage and Family Therapy, with a specialization in Child and Adolescent Therapy, which led me to my next job at a community counseling and meditation center in central Ohio.

There, I worked as a marriage and family therapist (MFT). I had clients from all walks of life. Some of them were wealthy entrepreneurs, some were criminals. I saw white people, black people, and many people from other ethnic and cultural backgrounds, too. I treated kids and elderly people, as well. The people I worked with there were truly diverse.

The majority of my caseload consisted of couples and families. Most of the couples attended therapy voluntarily, and others were mandated to attend by court authority. The court-ordered clients typically were sent to treatment as a stipulation to receive parenting rights or joint custody; some court-ordered clients were sent in for anger management classes— and on occasions, substance abuse group therapy.

Most of the clients I saw had problems with anxiety or depression. A lot of them had no idea that the strong uncomfortable feelings they felt daily were actually diagnosable mental illnesses. Had they never received treatment, they most likely would have continued to suffer. Many of them were trapped in a downward spiral, and therapy meaningfully redirected the downward trajectory of their lives.

The experiences I've had (and the observations I have made) during my journey as a mental health practitioner compelled me to write this book to increase mental health awareness to alleviate the impact that mental health issues have on black and brown communities.

Breakdown of *Black Mental Health Matters*

This book is divided into three sections. The first part touches on common misconceptions people have about mental health. The second part is going to discuss topics in our community that have a significant influence on mental health, like poverty, substance abuse, and race. These are typical problems in the black community but are rarely mentioned in the same breath with mental illness. The goal of section two is to bridge the gap in our understanding of how these issues affect our mental health. The third section will touch on diagnosable mental illnesses such as major depressive disorder, generalized anxiety disorder, and posttraumatic stress disorder. Also, in the third section, there will be vignettes to demonstrate how each illness plays out in real life.

What is Mental Health, and Why Does it Matter?

Mental Health refers to a wide range of conditions that affect our thoughts, mood, and even our behavior; it is an essential component of our overall wellbeing. Our minds guide our functioning in all aspects of life. Many people don't recognize the connection between emotional stability and other areas of life. The truth of the matter is that our emotional state is way more influential than we realize. Think about it this way; if you're dealing with immense psychological stress, it can be challenging to perform efficiently in other areas of life.

For instance, a nerve-wracking situation at home, like relationship problems or the loss of a loved one, can carry over into work by negatively impacting your performance or relationship(s) with co-workers. Yes, it's true, your co-worker who is always being a dick is probably going through something and isn't dealing with it constructively.

On the other hand, your work life can cause problems at home. Toxic employers constantly criticizing your work performance, or petty office drama can lead to depression or social anxiety disorder.

The average person doesn't know much about mental health. Most people only have a vague understanding of it. How many times have you heard someone called *bipolar* because they can't make up their

mind, or because of their unpredictable attitude? Although such behavior may describe bipolar disorder to an extent, that is far from a full
description of bipolar disorder.

What about depression? Everyone has heard of it, but most of us
really don't know what it is. So often, we describe ourselves or someone
else as depressed because we're upset. Of course, sadness is the most
distinctive feature of depression, but depression has many other, more
subtle symptoms, some of which, to accurately diagnose, require a
thorough examination by a mental health practitioner.

We call folks psycho, schizophrenic, OCD, and so on, all of which
are actually legitimate mental health terms and diagnosable illnesses.
We tend to minimize psychological disorders because we don't understand them, and use nicknames or epithets for things that people do,
think, or say. On top of a lack of knowledge about mental illnesses,
people, in general, have a limited understanding of mental health
treatment. This unfamiliarity is especially widespread in lower-income
societies— primarily black and brown communities.

That is not to say that the lack of knowledge is indicative of inherent inferiority, but it does suggest that those who are in power severely
neglect black and brown communities. People of color are mistreated
concerning schooling, housing, protection by (and in many cases,
from) police, employment, and many other basic human needs—mental health care is no exception.

Public school administrators and teachers regularly overlook the
signs of mental health illnesses, too. And police officers and judges
usually misunderstand mental illnesses, treating them as criminal behavior, especially when it comes to black and brown people. Far too
often, individuals with mental disorders don't get the help they need
from local government organizations.

Over the past few years, there's been a lot of talk about mental
health, but still, plenty of people have no idea what mental health is—
let alone how mental health treatment can change their lives for the
better. Not knowing is one of the main reasons people don't get the
right type of help.

Also, people in our community go to religious leaders for help with emotional issues, instead of going to a therapist or a doctor. Their decision to do so is a prime example of not recognizing that other, scientifically proven options are available. People within this school of thought believe we can just pray about psychological disorders, and they will go away.

There are all sorts of religious principles that support the misunderstanding that mental health disorders are different from other types of illnesses. It seems like religious people think we should be able to get over our mental health problems by ourselves, without any professional assistance. Yet, few people entertain the idea of "just getting over" physical illnesses like diabetes or heart disease without the help of a trained medical practitioner.

How often have you heard the saying, "too blessed to be stressed?" As if you cannot have blessings and stressors simultaneously. Sometimes emotional issues can be more problematic than physical ailments, so why would someone not utilize their best options to eliminate the problem? The answer is simple—they don't know any better! They attempt just about everything to cure themselves—except the methods which are backed by scientific data—like going to see a therapist. As illogical as these methods for solving mental illnesses are, in our community, these are the most common approaches to deal with them.

Another reason mental health is rarely addressed is that people are embarrassed. They feel like their problems are unique, and others won't be able to identify with their struggles. The truth is most of us—whether we realize it or not—have (or have had) the same problems. People see visiting a therapist, or even considering mental health services, as an admittance of weakness or inadequacy, which tends to turn into embarrassment.

The shame that one feels about seeing a counselor or taking medication occurs because of the *stigma* society has created surrounding mental illness. Stigma is a mark of shame or disgrace based on a characteristic or circumstance. There are two basic types of mental illness stigmas: social stigma, which is the discriminatory behavior and prejudicial attitudes people have toward those with mental illnesses, and self-stigma, which is due to the negative feelings people have about themselves based on what society has been feeding them. Often, the stigma is what pushes people further away from getting help.

Many people don't even entertain the idea of getting help because they're afraid of being labeled as "crazy" or some other derogatory term. In addition to the fear of alienation, quite a few misconceptions and myths about mental illness and mental health treatment stop people from seeking help from a trained practitioner, some of which will be discussed in the upcoming chapters.

Myths about Mental Illness and Mental Health Treatment

Therapy is only for crazy people

It is widely believed that therapy is *only* for those who are psychologically unstable. Although an emotionally unstable person's best chance at achieving stability is, indeed, through treatment from a trained professional, people without severe problems attend therapy as well.

Couples dealing with infidelity, parents of defiant children, or those grieving the loss of a loved one all can benefit from the help of a therapist. Truthfully, all types of people come to therapy for a variety of issues. In my honest opinion, it's "crazier" to avoid treatment—knowing you might need it—than to attend a therapy session (or multiple sessions) and sort out whatever issues you have.

As I mentioned earlier, in many cases it is the stigma associated with mental illness that tends to prolong things. People cut themselves off from the appropriate solutions to solve their problems out of fear of being judged negatively. If that describes you, think about it this way, would you think someone was terminally ill if he or she went to the doctor for a check-up? Or would you believe a friend was mentally challenged if he or she had a tutor in school? Absolutely not! It would be unreasonable to jump to those conclusions based on such inadequate evidence. Therefore, this begs the question: Why do we make such thoughtless judgments about getting help with our mental health, knowing good and got-damn well we need it?

The therapist will judge me...

Learning to project a nonjudgmental attitude is a part of every practitioner's training. In my experience, most therapists can separate their personal views from their dealings with clients. Believe it or not, the majority of therapists are somewhat numb to the issues clients bring into therapy. That's not to say they don't care, it's just that they have a professional view of your problems. They're not looking at your situation in the same way people on the street would look at it. Therapists are way less judgmental than the average person.

It is unlikely there are problems a therapist hasn't seen and treated several times before. However, I will say that mental health professionals are human—and they have personal values and principles—but they have a professional obligation not to bring their biases into treatment. Look at it this way—do you think your doctor will judge you if you had a disease, or would your lawyer judge you over legal matters, probably not.

Only weak-minded people need treatment

This is probably the misconception I hear the most. It is also the most untrue. In my opinion, culture is the main contributor to this myth. Most people in the United States—especially people within disenfranchised black and brown communities—have little experience with mental health treatment. So, they don't really know what type of people see counselors, therapists, psychologists, and other mental health practitioners.

The only experience most people have with mental health treatment is through television shows like *The Sopranos*, with Tony Soprano, stretched out on a leather sofa venting to his psychologist; or *The Fresh Prince of Bel-Air*, when Will and Lisa went to marriage counseling and ended up getting in a foam baseball-bat fight with an elderly couple. But maybe the most outrageous representation of therapy on television is from shows like *Dr. Phil* or *Marriage Boot Camp*, where talk-show therapists berate and embarrass their guests, and argue with anyone who disagrees with their advice.

These types of shows give the impression that therapists are condescending know-it-alls that shame you into recovery. That said, many people fear therapy and associate the very thought of needing treatment with an admission of weakness. However, the truth is that seeking mental health treatment is an exemplary demonstration of emotional maturity. It is an indicator that a person has accepted the fact that he or she needs help and is willing to take the necessary steps to take care of himself or herself.

People from virtually every walk of life attend therapy for a variety of reasons. I have counseled doctors, lawyers, and CEOs, as well as blue-collar and low-income people. Individuals of every race, ethnicity, socioeconomic status, sexual orientation, and religion can benefit from mental health treatment.

Getting help for mental health makes you appear no weaker than getting help for any other personal matter. Most people who go to therapy or take medications are regular people who live ordinary lives. But, no one, no matter how strong, is exempt from mental illnesses. Therefore, we must stop viewing these issues as something that only happens to certain people. Mental illnesses are actually more common than medical conditions like asthma. As a matter of fact, one in five adults in the U.S. experiences mental illness in any given year. Whereas one in thirteen people in the U.S. has asthma. I say this not to minimize the seriousness of asthma, but to highlight how common mental illnesses are.

No one will understand the issues I have

Even though mental illnesses like major depression or generalized anxiety are widespread, people still think they're alone in their battle with these illnesses. Although the root causes of the many psychiatric disorders listed in the DSM-5 (Diagnostic and Statistical Manual of Mental Health Disorders, fifth edition) vary, the symptoms are mostly universal.

For example, the cause of generalized anxiety disorder (GAD) may be different from person-to-person (e.g., biological predisposition or situation-dependent), but the symptoms of GAD are basically the same for everyone, with minor differences. In other words, the origin of the disorder varies, but everyone who's diagnosed has the same symptoms.

Yes, some people may have a different combination of symptoms. One person might worry a lot and have headaches during the day. And another person might worry at night and have sleep problems. Both have anxiety, just a different combination of symptoms. No one is better suited to understand the complex nature of these issues than a therapist. You'd be surprised how much they actually understand your situation. That said, you can bet that through years of experience and training, your therapist knows the ins and outs of your condition.

There is no difference between therapy and talking with a friend you can trust

I cannot tell you how many times my personal advice to a family member or friend has been mistaken as me trying to "Psychoanalyze" them. Of course, this misunderstanding is mainly because I am a therapist, and apparently, my friends and family believe I love my job so much that I perform psychiatric interventions on anyone I come into contact with who is experiencing an emotional issue. I say this jokingly, but it is not uncommon for people to be unfamiliar with what a therapist does.

The main reason people mistake my advice for therapeutic intervention is many people think that therapy is, in a nutshell, just a conversation in which the therapist gives advice.

Often, people expect counselors to be incredibly wise individuals with infinite knowledge who have the answers to all of life's problems. So, when issues arise, this assumption is usually the justification behind *choosing not* to visit a counselor; people believe that a wise friend is an adequate substitute for a trained mental health practitioner.

The problem with this sort of thinking is that it's a misunderstanding of the role of the counselor in relation to how they help clients. It is not the counselor's job to have a profound reply to every inquiry. No one in the world knows the answer to every problem—so, it is unreasonable to expect a counselor to be the exception. But they do have specialized knowledge about mental health issues that an untrained person does not.

Another key difference between seeing a trained professional and venting to a friend is that a friend is less likely to "tell it like it is" because doing so might damage their friendship with that person.

Sometimes, our friends want, so badly, to help us through tough times that they actually miss the opportunity to help. Our friends have personal relationships with us that make it impossible for them to have a neutral viewpoint of the issue at hand, which makes it probable that our friend may not recognize how we contribute to the dysfunction in our lives.

Conversation is only the surface level of therapy. The belief that therapy is *just* a counselor-client discussion in which the therapist gives advice is a gross distortion of the truth. Counselors undergo several years of education and real world training to learn how to dissect and effectively treat emotional problems. Counselors use systematic approaches and apply skillful tactics that are proven to help clients make necessary changes in their lives.

People with mental illnesses are violent

Perhaps the most stereotypical perception of people with mental illnesses is that they are dangerous or unpredictable. Only 3-5% of violent acts—including shootings— in the U.S. are due to mental illness. In fact, people with mental disorders are 12 times more likely to be victims of violent crime than the general U.S. population[1]. Most people with mental illnesses are rarely violent. However, people with serious mental illness are at high risk of violence during high-risk periods, such as the first episode of psychosis (psychosis refers to conditions in which there has been some loss of contact with reality).

I don't have any mental health problems; I would know if I had an issue.

Even if they realize that they are not feeling emotionally well, most people who have a mental disorder don't actually know they have an *illness*. Very few people—outside of practitioners—know the symptoms of even the most common mental illnesses, let alone the rarer and complex conditions such as borderline personality disorder, or oppositional defiant disorder.

It's alarming how many people are living with mental illnesses without knowing. So many folks experience suicidal thoughts, a loss of interest in once-pleasurable activities, appetite changes, and sleep problems—without even realizing they meet the criteria for major depressive disorder.

Depression (or any mental illness, for that matter) is something we don't talk about enough in our community—so, of course, the average person wouldn't recognize the signs or symptoms.

I've been to therapy before, and it didn't work.

After having bad prior experience(s) in therapy, people usually associate their specific experience(s) with therapy in general. They make the mistake of thinking of therapy as a one-size-fits-all type of treatment. There are no guarantees in therapy. No therapist is successful with every client. Aside from incompetence (which is not often the case), the reason therapy does not work is usually because of a lack of rapport between the therapist and the client.

Simply put, the therapist's style of therapy and personality sometimes are not a match with the client's personality or treatment expectations. To an extent, it's kind of like that saying we always hear in boxing: "styles make fights." In other words, some therapists are a good fit for some people and not for others.

It's likely that one of the following is true about people who have had unhelpful therapy experiences: (a) they were counseled by an incompetent therapist or (b) the client and the therapist were just not a good fit. All in all, plenty of reasons can cause a person to have a bad experience in therapy, but one thing I can say for sure is that each therapist is different, and it's in your best interest to "shop around" for the therapist that best fits you.

Our Environment and Our Mental Health Impact Each Other

Countless societal factors can lead to—or worsen—someone's mental health. It is reasonable to say that everyone—regardless of race or social class—has circumstances within their environment that are potentially harmful to their emotional wellbeing. However, due to a legacy of oppression, the number of *risk factors* for mental illness and emotional turmoil is disproportionately greater for people living in black and brown communities.

Risk factors include circumstances such as poverty, community violence, and substance abuse, all of which increase an individual's vulnerability to mental illness. Often, the problems that stem from risk factors overlap and create more complex problems that tend to take precedence over mental health matters in social, cultural, and legal spheres. The connection between risk factors and mental illness is called *intersectionality.* In this section, we will explore some of the most pervasive factors in our community that negatively influence our mental health.

Issues that Increase the Risk for Developing a Mental Health Disorder

Race

> *"At the root of this dilemma is the way we view mental health in this country. Whether an illness affects your heart, your leg or your brain, it's still an illness, and there should be no distinction."*
>
> *–Michelle Obama*

The inner-cites of America, such as Southside Chicago, North Philly, South Central Los Angeles, Baltimore, and Detroit—as well as many others—are plagued by risk factors that increase the potential for its residents to develop mental illnesses, such as major depressive disorder, or posttraumatic stress disorder (PTSD). These inner-city areas are heavily populated with black and brown people, which means that people of color have a higher likelihood of having psychological disorders. According to the Health and Human Services Office of Minority

Health, African-Americans are 20% more likely to develop mental health issues than the general population.

Black people are at the bottom of nearly every statistic that measures quality of life. This does not mean that black people are inherently inferior or that they don't try as hard to succeed in life as others do. Nor does this mean the system is broken, as I often hear people say. What it means is the system has done exactly what it was designed to do—keep black people in a primitive and docile state, to benefit those who are in power.

The absence of mental health awareness in our community is nothing more than a result of years and years of oppression—the same could be said about financial literacy—therefore, we need to increase our mental health literacy. We cannot afford to wait any longer. We cannot wait for the government, an athlete, or an entertainer to speak up and offer a solution to our problems, WE HAVE TO BE THE SOLUTION!

Common Sense Really Ain't that Common...

One of the main reasons the rate of mental illness in African-American communities is so high is because there is a lack of awareness concerning the signs, symptoms, and treatment options available for people with mental disorders. We rely too often on "common sense" to deal with serious emotional issues, which usually does not help at all. Common sense really isn't all that common. Because if it were, more black people would be open to getting help.

We call upon our cousins, besties, and even our parents to help us through tough situations. But truthfully, our loved ones simply aren't well equipped to deal with complex marital problems or severe mental disorders. The average person most likely doesn't even know where to start. Besides, many don't know the signs of a condition like depression or bipolar disorder. They may know what it feels like, but do they recognize the symptoms of mental illness when they see them? Can they describe them? Being able to do so is important when it comes to knowing when you or someone else needs help.

Clinical intervention is needed to overcome depression. It does not just go away! If you notice yourself or someone else experiencing the signs of depression (which will be discussed later in the book), don't wait, act now, and get some help.

Ignorance at its height

When I was younger, growing up on the east side of Detroit, I lived down the street from a group home that housed men and women who were severely mentally ill (by the way, "mentally ill" is not a derogatory term, as many people mistakenly believe). Some of the people in the group home were *Schizophrenic*. People with Schizophrenia see and hear things that are not real (hallucinations). They have strange beliefs that most of us know for a fact aren't true (delusions). Those with a limited understanding of mental illness are frightened, annoyed, and sometimes amused by Schizophrenics.

In my neighborhood, the group home was known as the "crazy house" because, to us, the residents acted "crazy." We didn't understand that those people were sick. All we knew was that they were grown-ups walking up the street, talking to themselves, and wearing weird clothes. One man would wear five pairs of pants, a long-sleeve shirt, three short-sleeve shirts, shorts on top of pants, two hats, shades, and mix-matched shoes. All in the summer heat! And I don't know how he did it, but he never wore the same thing twice. It was remarkable.

Looking back, I feel bad, though, because we would tear his ass up! I mean, he wouldn't even make it two steps out the house without an onslaught of cruel jokes from what seemed like the whole neighborhood. But in all fairness, he usually would joke back at us. I don't know if it was because he was thick-skinned or just out of touch with reality, but he never seemed all that bothered by our comments.

Kids, and even adults, too, make fun of things they don't understand. I feel that if we really understood what the residents at that group home were going through, we would have been more compassionate.

When it comes to mental illness, lack of understanding — which often precedes a lack of compassion—isn't uncommon within our community. Hopefully, by the time you finish reading this book, you will have a newfound, empathetic outlook on people who have mental illnesses.

Prayer Warriors Can't Replace Therapists

Religious views also separate many blacks from seeking treatment. Our culture is notorious for replacing therapy with prayer. When problems arise, many religious folk rely on scripture to see them through. By no means, am I bashing anyone's beliefs; spirituality can be instrumental in getting through tough times. However, even a prayer from Bishop T.D. Jakes, himself, can't replace treatment from a trained therapist. I hate to say it, but you can't just pray away a mental ailment, like PTSD, no more than you can pray away a broken leg.

There is a sector within the black church community known as "prayer warriors." Prayer warriors are highly spiritual people who are committed to praying for others. If you know church folks, you have heard people call on the prayer warriors to help them during trying times.

I think we all have seen a social media post or two (or a hundred) saying, "I need all my prayer warriors to help me out on this one…" Or a simple, "pray for me" without giving any details as to what we're praying for. I can't help but wonder how many of those calls for prayer were related to a problem best suited for a therapist. If I were a betting man, I'd say a lot.

Culturally Misunderstood…

Misdiagnosis is a significant barrier to mental health treatment for black and brown people. Of course, therapists—just as almost any other professionals—sometimes get diagnoses wrong. Due to our minority status, it's likely, the people we go to for help (doctors, lawyers, psychologists, etc.) are from a different cultural background. Which means they probably don't understand African-American social dynamics. Counselors that are not knowledgeable about black culture may not sufficiently understand specific problems—or even simple commonalities that are unique to the black community.

People tend to mistake certain cultural norms as dysfunctional behavior. This is especially true when it comes to black people. If you think about it, nearly everything that is "black" at its core, traditional or customary in the black community is stigmatized in some way. Our names: *Lakeisha, Daquan, Diamond* are deemed as ghetto. Our hair, the way it naturally grows out of our head, is considered unprofessional. And hair texture unlike ours is seen as "good hair." Even the way we talk—Ebonics, or African-American vernacular— is often made out to be inadequate.

I've known colleagues to misdiagnose black children because they misread cultural behaviors. One of my earliest experiences with misdiagnosis involved an African-American teen who was referred by his school to the agency I was working with to get treatment for insubordination.

The child was a high school freshman, and a known "class clown," who obnoxiously "flamed" or "roasted" his classmates (and the teacher) daily, which led to several schoolyard fights and suspensions.

The therapist assigned to treat the boy—a white, middle-aged woman—diagnosed him with oppositional defiant disorder (ODD), which is a disorder characterized by hostile, rebellious, and vindictive behavior. Granted, almost everyone could agree that he had behavioral problems—except for his friends who encouraged him to act up—yet, it's still a clear misinterpretation to perceive roasting as meeting the criteria for ODD.

Kids with ODD are typically less playful, more disorderly, spiteful, and argumentative than this boy was. He just talked entirely too much and was seeking attention. It is typical for teenage black boys to laugh at and crack jokes on one another to gain popularity in school settings. To someone that is not of the culture or at least knowledgeable of the culture, it is easy to misconstrue this black teenager's behavior as something much more severe, like ODD. Far too often, I've seen common, minor transgressions (like roasting) of school-aged black children be misinterpreted as hostility or aggression. Mistaken cultural nuance is one of the main factors in the misdiagnosis of black people, and this trend is why a lot of black people have reservations about getting mental health treatment.

Don't Judge a Book by its Cover

Although it's probable mental health practitioners from different cultural backgrounds may not understand the nuances of our culture, it is impossible to know that before meeting them. Therefore, it behooves you to meet with the practitioner before making any decisions. I say this because people often assume therapists of different races or backgrounds will not understand their problems.

Then again, people tend to assume therapists of the same race or background will be a better fit, which is not always the case. While these are fair assumptions (and often valid), you'd be surprised by how many clients have strong therapeutic relationships with therapists from different cultures. If the practitioner is skillful and compassionate, he or she will be able to help—regardless of their personal background.

We Don't Trust Y'all

For many, the first and only counseling experience they've had is through the courts. That said, a lot of black folks are distrustful of therapy in general. People fear that the information they share with a counselor may be used against them in the court of law, or will land them in a mental institution.

Truthfully, there are some instances where the information disclosed during treatment may have consequences. Nearly all mental health professionals are *mandated reporters*, which means they have a legal obligation to report situations in which clients are dangerous to themselves or others. So, if a therapist is notified, or has reasonable suspicion to believe, that a client is planning on committing suicide or a murder, abusing children or elders, he or she must report to the appropriate authority what they know or reasonably suspect.

You Have Rights to Privacy

Aside from situations in which the counselor is required by law to report, everything that is said or done in therapy is entirely confidential, meaning the therapist can be held accountable by the law for sharing any details from your case without your express written consent to do so.

The Health Insurance Portability and Accountability Act of 1996 (HIPAA) is a set of rules to protect the privacy of mental health patients. Because of HIPPA, therapists are strictly prohibited from providing any information about you to anyone without your consent. You don't have to worry that a casual visit to see your counselor would lead to you being admitted into a psychiatric ward, or being brought up on criminal charges. After all, a therapist's job is to help you, not get you in trouble with the law, or make your life harder.

Make a Difference

Mental health treatment in black and brown communities is rare, and there's minimal social and community support for people who need help with psychological problems. The combination of stigmatization, along with the illness itself, is devastating.

Mental illnesses already have a way of making you feel alone. Imagine being pushed away by your family and friends during times when you need them the most. Picture being rejected for problems that are beyond your control, as if you're only experiencing these problems because you're somehow weaker than, or not as smart as, everyone else. If those thoughts don't feel good to you, then they probably don't feel too enjoyable to others either. Instead of bashing, be supportive. Make a difference in someone's life.

To some of you reading this book, these may be circumstances you know very well, whether it's from personal experience or observation of others. Either way, we must not denounce those who need help. Understanding and addressing mental health will help improve the quality of life for individuals and families within our community, which will in turn, advance the community as a whole.

Mental illnesses associated with race:

- Major depressive disorder
- Generalized anxiety disorder
- Social anxiety
- Posttraumatic stress disorder

Substance abuse

"Addiction begins with the hope that something 'out there' can instantly fill up the emptiness inside."

–Jean Kilbourne

It's common knowledge that mental illness goes hand-in-hand with *substance abuse*. Substance abuse is excessive use of a drug. It is a pervasive issue amongst every race, including blacks. You'd be hard-pressed to find a community where drugs aren't a problem. People often resort to abusing drugs, alcohol, or other addictive substances during tough times. This is primarily because many people lack sufficient coping skills to manage life's adversities.

Rarely does society take into consideration the backstory of substance abusers. We see people doing drugs —like there is no tomorrow—without ever really questioning what circumstances contributed to them using. It is as if we think addiction happens within a vacuum, and the person you see on the corner, strung out, is naturally that way. As if they were never anything other than a drunk, a crackhead, a junkie, or whatever other derogatory names we apathetically give to addicted people.

Several circumstances give rise to substance abuse, but mental illness is the leading contributor. About 50% of people with mental illnesses also have issues with drugs, and 37% of alcoholics have at least one other psychiatric disorder. Also, more than half of drug abusers (53%) have a mental disorder.[2]

These stats indicate there is a strong connection between mental illness and substance abuse. Although not commonly referred to as such, substance abuse, itself, is considered a mental illness. Having more than one mental illness at the same time is called *comorbidity*. For instance, a person living with depression who is also addicted to heroin is considered comorbid because he or she has two co-existing disorders. People suffering from both addiction and mental problems need to address their substance abuse issues first. It's widely believed in the psychotherapy field that mental health treatment is ineffective when substance abuse is unaddressed.

Emotional Origins of Addiction

Many people use drugs as an attempt to alleviate the symptoms of mental illness. In other words, they use them to numb the pain. This type of behavior is called *self-medication*. Someone who is depressed might use cocaine as an upper (a stimulant that increases energy and alertness) to balance sad, lethargic, negative moods; another person's drug of choice might be opioids, for their calming effect, as a means to silence anger from a traumatic past.

Self-mediators are looking to fill a void. Whether it's to avoid specific negative feelings, to give themselves a boost of something they're lacking (i.e., confidence, energy, or a positive mood), or to deal with something that's already happened; there's usually some underlying psychological cause for their excessive drug use.

The mental illness/addiction conversation is the same as the chicken and the egg: no one knows which comes first. Does the mental illness cause drug abuse, or does the drug abuse cause mental illness—or is it a mixture of both? The world may never know. Regardless, one thing can be said for sure, both are a big issue in the black community.

It Runs in The Family

Intergenerational substance abuse (substance abuse that is passed from generation-to-generation) is a considerable risk factor for addiction. Our parents' problems with addiction are a great predictor of difficulties to come for later generations. Of course, this is not always the case. Sometimes individuals with substance abusing families manage to abstain from drugs and alcohol. However, our parents, grandparents, and other significant caregivers are influential when it comes to addiction. I am by no means insinuating we are not responsible for our own behaviors, but I'd be remiss not to mention the role our parents' abuse plays. If I had a dollar for every time I heard a client say "my mama was a crackhead" or "my daddy was an alcoholic" or how their "OG" got them started with smoking weed, I'd be set for life!

Almost every person I met who dabbled in drugs or alcohol was influenced by a parent or a parental figure. Either it was directly witnessing them use, or it was the ramifications of their usage, such as parents not assuming an appropriate parental role (i.e., being more of a friend than a parent); unsuitable child-rearing strategies like excessive whoopings; or just all-out chaos and drama that didn't foster abstention from drugs.

It's difficult to sufficiently raise a child if a parent is getting high or drunk every day. As a matter of fact, while addicted to drugs or alcohol, it's nearly impossible to consistently do just about any task that requires effort or responsibility, let alone raise and provide a stable home for a child. Therefore, it's no wonder an overwhelming majority of substance abusers come from homes in which the parental figures were addicts—they're simply part of a vicious cycle.

Genetics Play a Role Too

Along with unstable homes contributing to the development of a substance abuse disorder, genetics are also a factor. Studies show that people with substance abuse problems have deficiencies in certain parts of their brain. There are three main parts of the human brain: the *cerebrum, cerebellum,* and *brain stem.*

The cerebrum is the largest part of the brain and fills up most of your skull. It's responsible for memory, problem solving, thinking, and feeling. The cerebellum is in the back of your head; it controls your balance and coordination. And beneath the cerebrum, in front of the cerebellum, is the brain stem; it connects the brain to the spinal cords and controls your automatic functioning (the things you do without conscious effort), such as your heart rate, breathing, digestion, and blood pressure.

Within the cerebrum, there is an area called the frontal lobe that controls the brain's *executive functions* (i.e., memory, self-control, reasoning, attention, problem solving). The term "executive function" is a business metaphor, suggesting that your brain's executive functions work similarly to the way a CEO manages all of a company's different departments so the company can operate as efficiently as possible.

How we organize our lives, how we plan, and how we then perform those plans is mainly guided by our executive system. People with deficits in executive functioning tend to be impulsive, have difficulty planning for future events, behave in socially inappropriate ways, and have a lack of awareness regarding problem areas in their lives, which makes them susceptible to drug abuse and alcoholism.

Mental illnesses associated with substance abuse:

- Major depressive disorder
- Generalized anxiety disorder
- Posttraumatic stress disorder
- Antisocial personality disorder

Suicide

"The bravest thing I ever did was continuing my life when I wanted to die."

—Juliette Lewis

Suicide is one of the most—if not the most—devastating effects of mental illness. Most people who commit suicide could no longer deal with the pain of mental illness. Roughly, 90% of people who take their own lives had a mental disorder, with depression and substance abuse being the most common examples.

Given the high number of mentally ill people who commit suicide, it's reasonable to assume that a large number of them did not receive proper attention. I wonder how many of the 90% were dealing with depression in silence. Only God knows how many would've pulled through if they'd had more support. I can only imagine how many of them didn't really want to die, and were just trying to end the suffering. The most frustrating part about this is they probably didn't realize they weren't crazy, and death wasn't the answer. Most importantly of all, they weren't alone.

Suicide is rarely spoken about in the black community. People in general—and minorities in particular—view suicide as a "white people problem," which is expected, seeing that white people have the highest suicide rate amongst all races in the US per capita.

African-Americans make up approximately 12% of the United States. Fifty-three percent of the African-American population is female. At birth, men outnumber African-American women. But by the time black men reach the 15 to 24 age group, the pattern is reversed, and women begin to outnumber men.

The decline in the black male population is due to homicide, addiction, and, surprisingly—suicide. The fact that most suicides we hear about involve people who don't look like us can make suicide seem like a distant issue. It's no wonder blacks dismiss the importance of talking about it.

Traditionally, blacks have had lower suicide rates than whites and other races across all age groups. Nevertheless, new research has shown that black youth are at a much higher risk of suicide than ever before.

Our Precious Children are at Risk

The suicide rate of black children under the age of 13 is twice as high as that of white kids in the same age group. To my understanding, the high suicide rates amongst this age group are mainly due to developmental issues and possibly a lack of family emotional support.

With social media and other advancements in technology, kids are more socially isolated today than ever. Today's children don't have the real face-to-face support that you might have had growing up. Also, many kids do not have the wisdom to manage stressful situations like bullying or sexual assault, and their brains are not fully developed (unlike adults who have reached their peak developmentally), which makes them more susceptible to mental health issues after emotionally challenging situations.

What makes matters worse—as if the fact that precious black kids have the highest suicide rate amongst their age group isn't enough—is the fact that these kids who are experiencing problems are not being talked to enough about their issues, as older kids are, because parents believe that it is "too much" to speak to young children about suicide.

We, as parents, must understand that it is never too early to talk to a child about suicide—especially if that child has been through a traumatic situation. We must open all lines of communication about mental health with our children, as we are their first line of defense when it comes to being open about how they feel about themselves, others, and the world in general. It's in our best interest to let our children know that no conversation, including suicide, is off-limits.

In 2017, there was a study conducted that showed children age 5 to 11, and young adolescents from 12 to 14 who committed suicide were most likely to be male, African-American, and dealing with stressful relationships at home or with friends[3]. The study suggested young children who were formally diagnosed at the time of their death, were more likely to have been diagnosed with attention deficit hyperactivity disorder (ADHD), while the young adolescent group was more likely to have been diagnosed with depression.

While not every child that commits suicide has ADHD, and not every adolescent who takes his or her own life is necessarily depressed, based on this research, it is reasonable to say that kids who have those diagnoses—and are going through rough patches with family or friends—are at risk for suicide.

There are countless reasons why people don't address suicide as much as they should. In my opinion, there are two main reasons why people don't talk about suicide: one being they don't recognize concrete signs of suicidal ideation; the other is people have incorrect beliefs about suicide itself. There are far too many myths about suicide, and people tend to gravitate towards those misconceptions.

Myths and Misconceptions about Suicide

Suicide, as with most mental health topics, is a concept the general population has little knowledge about. I think a big part of this discrepancy is because people who have experienced suicidal thoughts don't talk about it. The stigma of mental illness prevents people from even so much as mentioning they've thought about suicide because they don't want to be seen as crazy or overly dramatic.

Many people view the open expression of suicidal thoughts as attention seeking or being "extra." There's nothing "extra" about letting people know you're contemplating suicide. It's actually courageous, being vulnerable enough to let people know that you're not emotionally well and would like some help. As a matter of fact, it's ironic that most people who end up killing themselves do it because they feel helpless and alone. Imagine how many people would not take their lives if they had someone around them who saw the signs and intervened accordingly. False ideas and misunderstandings are what stand in the way of open discussions about suicide in the black community.

Myths versus Facts

Myths make up most of what is "understood" about suicide. And most of them were created from stereotypes. Much of the knowledge the general public has comes from people who know nothing about suicide. Suicide too serious of an issue to be misinformed about! It's okay not to know about sports or music. But it is absolutely necessary to have a solid understanding of suicide because such knowledge may be the difference between life and death for someone you love. Below are some of the most common myths about suicide.

Myth: *Talking about suicide is a bad idea because it will make someone actually try it.*

Fact: Suicide is a touchy subject. A lot of times, people don't want to bother others with how they feel, so they don't talk about it. And other times, they're just too embarrassed to bring things up on their own.

Directly asking someone about suicide gives the person permission to talk about how they feel. People who were suicidal have said that it was a huge relief to talk to someone about it. Once a person starts talking, they have a better chance of discovering alternative solutions to end the suffering, and death no longer seems like the best option.

Myth: *People who are suicidal want to die*

Fact: Most people who are suicidal don't want to die; they just don't want to live the life they're living. This distinction may be subtle, but it's critical, and is also the reason that talking about suicide at the right time is vital.

Myth: *Only people with mental illnesses commit suicide*

Fact: Not everyone who attempts or commits suicide is mentally ill. Most people with psychological disorders never experience suicidal thoughts.

31

There are plenty of reasons for someone to commit or attempt suicide. Relationship problems, life stressors, and/or trauma, such as sexual abuse, debilitating injuries, legal matters, rejection/embarrassment, and financial hardship can also push someone over the edge.

Myth: *Once a person is suicidal, they'll always be suicidal*

Fact: A large number of people who commit suicide have mental illnesses. With the proper treatment, suicidal ideation can be eliminated.

The act of suicide is an attempt to control deep, painful emotions and thoughts. Once these feelings disperse, so will the suicidal ideation. While suicidal thoughts can return, they are not permanent. With the right treatment, an individual with suicidal thoughts can live a long, happy, and successful life.

Myth: *People who commit suicide are selfish and are taking the easy way out.*

Fact: Typically, people don't kill themselves because they do not want to live —people die by suicide because they want to end their suffering. They are experiencing so much pain that they feel helpless and hopeless that their situation will ever change.

Individuals who suffer suicidal thoughts don't do so by choice. They are not just "thinking of themselves," but instead, they are going through a severe mental health crisis due to mental illness or a difficult life situation. Conditions such as depression can cause a person not to think rationally, making death seem like the only way out.

Myth: *Suicide happens suddenly without warning*

Fact: Warning signs—verbally or behaviorally—precede most suicides. It's an absolute must to learn them. Actually, learning the warning signs is an understatement—you should try to be an expert on suicidal ideation!

Those who are suicidal might only show warning signs to their friends and family. And loved ones may not recognize what's going on, which is why it seems like suicide happens without warning. So, I want to make it clear: it's absolutely vital to recognize the signs of suicidal ideation because knowing them can potentially save someone's life.

Risk Factors for Suicide

A suicide risk factor is a circumstance or characteristic of a person (or their environment) that makes it more likely (statically speaking) that they will die by suicide. Many people are at risk for suicide who never even think about killing themselves, let alone actually doing it. So, just because you or someone you know may be at risk doesn't mean that they have (or will have) issues with suicide, but it is in our best interest to know the risk factors because it gives us a sense of direction, in terms of circumstances, which lead to suicide, making us more prepared to intervene if necessary.

Risk Factors

Some of the most common risk factors for suicide are:

1. Family history of suicide
2. Family history of child mistreatment
3. History of suicide attempts
4. Mental illnesses (especially depression)
5. Substance abuse history
6. Access to lethal means (i.e., guns, pills, etc.)
7. Extreme loss (i.e., financial, loved ones, etc.)
8. Aggressive/impulsive tendencies

Signs of Suicidal Ideation

There are a lot of signs of suicidal ideation, so many that it's impossible to name all of them. Sadly, some suicide warning signs are so subtle that no one even notices. Imagine how easy it is for signs to go unnoticed if you don't know what to look for. We must equip ourselves with knowledge about suicide so that when symptoms are present, we're able to help. Suicidal ideation can be broken down into three categories: speech, behavior, and mood.

Someone who is suicidal may talk about:

- Killing themselves or talking about death more than they would normally
- Feeling hopeless
- Having no reason to live
- No one caring about them or being a burden to others
- Feeling trapped
- Unbearable emotional or physical pain

Behaviors that may signal risk, especially if related to a painful event, loss, or change:

- Increased use of alcohol and/or drugs
- Withdrawing from activities
- Socially isolated from friends and family
- Giving away prized possessions
- Increased aggression and irritation
- Sleeping too much or too little

People who are suicidal may display one or more moods:

- Extreme sadness
- Excessive worrying
- Loss of interest in hobbies

- Anger
- Humiliation or shame

Now that the risk factors and warning signs of suicide have been addressed, I want to provide you with the tools for intervening when someone is suicidal.

How to help someone that is suicidal

If you suspect someone is suicidal: Don't be afraid to ask if they're thinking about killing themselves. Be as straightforward as possible. This is not a time for shyness. We need to know right away if they're contemplating suicide because there may not be a later.

Encourage them to see a therapist, don't try to talk them out of suicide—let them know that the way they feel (key word: FEEL) is temporary. Feelings are not facts and are subject to change—especially with treatment from a trained professional. People who are suicidal simply need to know someone cares about their feelings, and that they are waiting for the opportunity to talk about their problems.

If you see the warning signs: Don't leave the person alone. If possible, ask for help from other friends or family members. Ask the person to give you any weapons he or she might have. Take away sharp objects or anything else they could use to hurt themselves. Try to keep them as calm as possible. Call 911 or take them to an emergency room. If they're already in psychiatric treatment, help him or her contact their doctor or therapist.

If you are contemplating suicide: Talk to someone you can trust. If you don't have anyone you can trust, seek help from a professional. If none of the above works, contact 911. At the end of the day, suicidal thoughts are temporary, and you don't want to make a permanent decision by committing suicide on temporary emotions. I know that may be easier said than done, but it can be done, and your life is worth fighting for.

We must act swiftly when someone is showing signs of suicidal ideation. With suicide, there is no time to waste, every moment counts. We can't afford to be passive about it. We cannot wait for the right time to talk about suicide—because there is no right time. Right away is always the best time to ask about suicide.

Mental illnesses associated with suicide:

- Nearly every mental illness has a connection to suicide.

Marital Problems

"It is not a lack of love, but a lack of friendship that makes unhappy marriages."

—Friedrich Nietzsche

Marriages are multifaceted relationships that combine romance, finance, family, and business. They can enhance a person's life in a variety of ways. However, when marriages are bad, they can seemingly make our lives a living hell.

In my experience, the most common issue discovered during marriage therapy is a lack of communication between partners. The way couples speak to each other is often more of a problem than the subjects they argue about. Poor communication seems to be the medium by which all—or mostly all—relationship problems occur. During heated discussions, both partners desperately try to get their point across, while basically ignoring the message their partner is trying to convey. To make matters worse, they tend to keep score about each other's transgressions to justify their anger and disrespect, which in turn, provides the other partner a rationale to be angry and disrespectful as well. This type of communication is a never-ending cycle, which usually leads to divorce or perpetual marital dissatisfaction—which often precedes or exacerbates mental illness.

Poor Communication Facilitating Poor Mental Health

Have you ever heard the saying, "It isn't what you say, but how you say it"? That statement is especially true when it comes to communicating with our spouses. Not only is it about how you say things, but it's also what you don't say, and what comments may emotionally trigger a partner—which may or may not—even be related to anything you've said or done.

Let me put it this way, sometimes silence speaks louder than words. And in many cases, not talking about situations leaves things up for interpretation—which is a recipe for disaster. No one, not even the most intuitive of people, can read someone's mind.

Sometimes, the problem in communication has very little to do with what is said, and more to do with emotional triggers or touchy subjects. Now, there is very little—if anything—you can do about triggering someone, especially if you are respectful in the way you are talking with them. That being the case, it's up to the listener to recognize they're being triggered by a situation from their past, and calm themselves.

So, you're probably wondering, *what the hell is an emotional trigger?* An emotional trigger is a situation that reminds someone of something upsetting from their past. Often, the emotional trigger has nothing to do with the situation at hand. That is why the emotional reaction from a triggered individual may seem—and often is—irrational.

For example, a couple I treated, Fernando and Marie, were arguing during a session about Marie feeling as though Fernando disrespects and undermines her authority in front of their children.

"Fernando, every time I tell the kids to do something, you always come behind me and tell them they don't have to do it!" Marie said.

Fernando replied in a frustrated and confused tone, "Aaren, I didn't say anything to undermine her, I swear to God! All I did was ask our son what she was yelling at him for. I had just come in from work and I heard her yelling. I just wanted to know what had happened."

Fernando may very well have undermined Marie's authority in the past, but I didn't sense that in this scenario. I got the feeling that Marie was holding onto something. She seemed to have been reminded of times in the past when she felt disrespected by Fernando and associated how she felt then with the current situation.

Because the emotional wounds from previous fights have yet to be resolved, they're still hurtful to Marie, which is why she gets upset by comments that are reminders of how she was treated before.

Do You Really Care for Me?

Emotional triggers are deeply rooted in what is referred to in the psychology world as "attachment." Basically, attachment is another word for emotional bonds or emotional security. Most of the time, when people are triggered emotionally, it's based on a violation of trust by someone who is (or was) a significant attachment figure.

This breach of trust is called an *attachment injury.* An attachment injury usually occurs in the form of serious betrayal—such as infidelity, domestic violence, or severe disrespect. Once a person experiences an attachment injury, they tend to have a hard time viewing the person who caused the damage as they did before—usually leading to perpetual feelings of resentment or distrust, causing them to be easily triggered.

Attachment is an intricate concept that's more of a theory than an absolute fact, but it's supported by scientific research, which makes it pretty reliable. Attachment is broken down into four styles: secure, anxious-preoccupied, dismissive-avoidant, and fearful-avoidant.

Each attachment style is based on early life experiences, dating back as far as infancy. Everyone has an attachment style. The styles are based on the relationship with our mother or primary caregiver when we were babies or toddlers. During the first two years of our lives, how our parents respond to us, mainly during times of distress, establishes the attachment pattern we form.

These patterns will go on to guide the child's feelings, thoughts, and expectations as an adult in future relationships. Our attachment styles are so relevant to the way we think that our brains code them as "safety." Any emotional distance (whether it is perceived or actual) in our close relationships is seen as a danger because losing connection to a loved one jeopardizes our sense of emotional security.

Once we feel our security is at risk, our bodies go into survival mode, setting off an alarm in the amygdala—the fear center of the brain. When the amygdala is triggered, our brain leaps into action to maintain connection or protect us from being hurt. This fight-or-flight response is what happens in relationships where one person is clingy or too distant. Over-pursuing or withdrawing is a typical example of someone trying to manage a challenge to their emotional security.

Attachment Styles are Interpretations of Emotional Safety

Our relationships—especially with significant others—are influenced by attachment style. Earlier, I briefly mentioned four basic attachment styles that are responsible for our perception of emotional security; there's secure attachment, which is the most healthy attachment style. And the other three are variations of insecure attachment, which is dysfunctional, but not necessarily completely bad. Other factors influence a person's ability to make connections, too, like life experiences or the attachment style of those he or she is connected with. Just because you have an insecure style doesn't mean you can't have meaningful relationships.

Attachment styles are how people define and obtain emotional safety. They typically begin in the first two years of our lives when we are highly dependent on our parents. This time period is influential in shaping how we seek connections. Securely attached individuals had close bonds with their caregivers, which helps them feel confident that they can make successful emotional connections.

Secure attachment is pretty straightforward—either you have a secure attachment style, or you don't. Insecure attachment is a little more complicated. There are different ways a person can have an insecure attachment style. One type of insecure attachment is anxious-preoccupied. People with this style are often viewed as clingy or needy. They have a strong desire for connection and fear abandonment. People with preoccupied attachment have had inconsistent or unreliable attachment figures.

Then there's dismissive-insecure. These people tend to be very dismissive of emotional needs—whether it be their own or others—hence the term "dismissive." Their seemingly nonchalant style of connecting is rooted in avoidance. Dismissive style people feel uncomfortable being vulnerable, so they stuff their emotions down and pretend they don't exist. People with this style had parents who were emotionally unavailable and made them feel bad for expressing themselves.

Last but not least, anxious-avoidant. Those with this attachment style usually have experienced some type of loss or trauma in childhood or adolescence. Anxious-avoidant people tend to avoid making close relationships out of fear of being hurt; they want to be close to others but find it difficult to trust people. People with anxious-avoidant attachment styles are like those with dismissive styles as they both avoid intimacy and suppress emotions as vulnerability is extremely uncomfortable to them.

Commitment issues can take over relationships

Sometimes people aren't quite ready to be locked down long-term, let alone for the rest of their lives. Commitment is a well-known problem among unmarried couples. Commitment issues are rooted in *attachment*.

For instance, an anxious-avoidant individual may be reluctant to commit out of fear of abandonment. Although abandonment is a legitimate concern for anyone, it holds more weight in the mind of someone with an anxious-avoidant style. But other factors affect commitment too, like immaturity, differences in expectations, and sometimes people just don't see a future in their relationship. At the end of the day, plenty of reasons may make a person slow to commit, and it takes a thorough assessment from a professional to get to the root of the issue.

Fear of Change

Time and time again, I've seen people who are afraid of losing their independence. People think once they get into a committed relationship, they'll lose their freedom, and their other half will become more like a probation officer than a spouse.

Believe me, I've seen my share of controlling partners who try to regulate their mate's every move. And I've heard stories about a night out with friends turning into an interrogation, like a scene from *The First 48*.

However, in most cases, people who struggle with commitment, misunderstand marriage: either they have an unrealistic expectation of what married life will be like, or they expect their lives to be exactly the same after marriage (which is also very unlikely). Either way, usually their assumptions are what cause ambivalence about tying the knot.

A couple I worked with years ago, Latasha and James, were in a relationship for six years, and James had yet to even considered marriage, which was incredibly frustrating for Latasha. In almost every session with them, the conversation somehow drifted to James' slowness to commit. So, I asked James, "What are your plans for this relationship, is marriage the long-term goal?"

James replied unconvincingly, "Yeah, that's the goal." Almost as if he were simply saying what he thought Latasha and I wanted to hear.

"So, if marriage is you all's long-term goal, how come you haven't popped the question?" I asked.

Latasha sarcastically interjected, "Yeah, what you waiting on?"

James started stuttering, "I... I... I'm just waiting on the right time, I guess."

James and Latasha are financially stable, as both have well-paying careers. They also have an eight-year-old daughter, and both agreed that marriage was, indeed, their long-term goal. But it seemed like the problem was what each partner deemed as the "right time" to get married.

Cold Feet Theory

In my experience, most people who want to get married but are, at the same time, hesitant to do so have this issue because they are in what I call the "cold feet" stage of a long-term relationship. Not everyone gets cold feet when it comes to long-term commitment, but for those who do, it's usually based on misconceptions of what married life will be like or that the person with the cold feet is not as interested in marriage as they claim.

Seeing all the boxes were checked for James' interest and investment in his relationship with Latasha—the disinterested part of my "cold-feet" theory could be ruled out. Therefore, I bluntly asked, "James, do you think you haven't popped the question yet because you're not done having fun yet, and marriage would end all the excitement in your life?"

James mumbled, "Yeah, that's right," like he was embarrassed to admit it.

I glanced over at Latasha, who was nodding her head and smiling as if she already knew how James felt but took pleasure in actually hearing him say the words. I also noticed a sense of relief in James' demeanor. It seemed like the weight of the world had been lifted from his shoulders because he finally realized—or at least admitted—what has been holding him back from doing what he wanted to do—marry Latasha.

In this scenario, James' unrealistic belief that marriage is going to kill the fun and excitement in his life is what prevented him from settling down. This thought is, for the most part, inaccurate because James has been living with Latasha and still having fun and enjoying his life for the past eight years; marriage—which is essentially a title and a piece of paper—won't prevent him from living an enjoyable and fulfilling life.

The Fantasy of the Perfect Man/Woman

To an extent, we all have expectations about the way future and current mates should be. We fantasize about their looks, their career, and even their personality. For some, these fantasies serve as a guideline or a set of standards to find someone that will make them happy. But others take the fantasy too far and end up sabotaging themselves from making meaningful connections.

Unrealistic expectations are such a common problem in couple's therapy that I expect to hear about them at some point during my time with all couples. These idealistic thoughts about what a husband/wife, girlfriend/boyfriend should be are problematic and usually lead to additional separate issues that add to the problems couples already have.

Many people go into a relationship expecting perfection from their partner while they, themselves, are anything but perfect! Perfection-seeking does nothing but cause resentment. One partner feels as if they are settling while the other thinks he or she is not good enough, or at least, their partner doesn't think so—which leads to more relationship problems.

If I had a dollar for every time a woman I was treating said that she wanted her man to have the looks of Idris Alba with the money and ambition of Diddy, I'd be a multimillionaire. And if I had a sandwich for every time a man said he wanted his woman to look like Rihanna, cook, clean, and make love on-demand, I'd be able to end world hunger.

People go into a relationship wanting perfection, or a fantasy type of relationship, and become discouraged, and even resentful, towards their partner when they don't get what they want.

I am not saying that we shouldn't have high standards, but one thing for sure is that we must understand there is another person in the relationship with us, who has their own wants, needs, values, and expectations. And not considering their wishes by only valuing our own is a recipe for disaster. After all, we are all a work in progress; to expect flawlessness is setting yourself up for failure.

Relationships are about BOTH people meeting the needs of the other, trading and exchanging equally, for shared balance and satisfaction, instead of trying to live up to unrealistic standards. Women are more than sex objects for men's physical pleasure, and men are more than status symbols for women's financial stability and personal validation. Unrealistic expectations can put a wedge in a couple's emotional comfort and closeness, leading to intimacy issues.

Intimacy Issues: the Byproduct of Relationship Dysfunction

When relationship problems arise, intimacy issues usually are not trailing too far behind. Intimacy issues are, for the most part, the result of a dysfunctional relationship. They typically come after infidelity, communication problems, abuse, or disrespect. Also, intimacy problems tend to be the precursor to most breakups.

Intimacy, for most people, means sexual activity. Even though sex is definitely an aspect of intimacy, it's nowhere near all there is to it. My personal definition of intimacy is to be emotionally close with someone, which is closer to the dictionary's description of it than the colloquial meaning. That said, a lot of people don't realize they are experiencing intimacy problems, and their relationship is seriously on the rocks because their sex life is still intact.

Intimacy issues are much subtler than we realize. I've seen couples that say they don't talk, and if they do, it's on a need-to basis. Some couples say that they don't feel emotionally safe with their partner, let alone communicating with them at an intimate level. When couples have intimacy issues, they attempt to mind-read, and to no one's surprise, assumptions are rarely correct, which gives way to a whole lot of other problems.

Mental illnesses associated with marital problems:

- Major depressive disorder
- Social anxiety disorder
- Generalized anxiety
- Bipolar disorder

Family Problems

"Family is supposed to be our safe heaven. Very often, it's the place where we find the deepest heartache."

—Iyanla Vanzant

Problems within the family system can be a significant contributor to mental health issues. I cannot stress enough how much the people we grow up around—especially our family—can affect our mental wellbeing.

Parents are the spearhead of emotional stability. Our early relationship with our parents is responsible for our attachment style. In addition to attachment style, our parents' personalities begin to shape our interpretation of the world. Parents (or any caregivers) are literally our first examples of how people behave, and how we learn our place in the world in relation to others.

So, if you grow up seeing your parents fighting, doing drugs, or exhibiting some other unhealthy behavior before you get a chance to get out into the world and see that those behaviors aren't typical, your parents' actions become normalized, and you begin to act in similar ways. Human beings are social learners. We learn from the people in our environment. The way you dress, your taste in food or music, how you talk, even the way you think is socially learned. Parents set the baseline for this social education; that's why it's imperative for parents to be positive role models for their children.

People who come from chaotic families, where fighting is the norm, tend to report mental illnesses the most. I don't even need to cite any statistical data to back up this claim; it would be a tall order trying to find a therapist that disagrees.

Emotionally unstable families facilitate mental illnesses. A person could acquire anxiety based on their dealings with a hostile or unpredictable mother. Another person could develop PTSD from a physically assaultive father, or perhaps depression, because they were teased maliciously by their siblings. Family issues run deep. Much of the time, the family of origin is where emotional problems start.

United We Stand, Divided We Fall

The emotional baggage parents bring into their marriage trickles down to their children. One way this can happen is through arguments between parents that are based on inconsistency and poor communication. An excellent example of this is one parent being too strict or one parent wanting to be best friends with the kids instead of a parent. These parenting difficulties lead to kids developing emotional or behavioral issues.

How can you expect a child to know how to behave if his parents are sending him mixed signals of what's acceptable behavior? You can't. One parent is telling him it's okay to act like a grownup, and the other treats him like a recruit in Marine boot camp. In these situations, the child gets confused and starts to behave the way he wants or follows the parent with the most influence, which isn't always in the child's best interest. Weak parental guidance is harmful to children, but absent, or inconsistent parents are even more damaging to a family's emotional development.

The Plight of Single Parent Families

Single-parent families are an epidemic in inner-city communities—especially black and brown neighborhoods. Why that is the case has been studied for decades. Some say it's because of a legacy of disenfranchisement of people of color, which has created a culture of single parenting. Others say it's a matter of poor choices that have led to generational cycles of unwed parents. Some believe the notion of single black parent ubiquity is a myth, perpetuated by stereotypes from racist media. Regardless, single-parent families are at risk for the development of emotional problems.

Plenty of at-risk children believe it's their fault that one of their parents isn't in the picture. Sometimes, this is because of the child's own dysfunctional thinking patterns, but other times it's because the present parent puts these ideas into the child's mind by badmouthing, or not talking about the other parent at all, which can be just as bad as slander.

As ridiculous it may seem, this idea of kids taking responsibility for their parent's absences isn't unusual—and certainly isn't entirely far-fetched on the child's part. If no one ever discusses the matter with the children, how can you reasonably expect them to understand why they only have one consistent parent?

Single parents are at-risk too. It takes a significant toll on someone's mental health to be solely responsible for a child that they didn't create by themselves. It's hard enough having to do this with help, so imagine what it's like for those who do it alone. There's a lot of potential for anxiety—from the instability of single-parenthood.

And there's also a risk for depression because single parents have to make many personal sacrifices. Job opportunities, romantic relation-ships, and even downtime are often forfeited, as raising children is the main priority for a lot of single parents. I'm not saying this is the case for everyone, but I'd bet there are many single parents who would agree with my assessment.

Because single parents do it all by themselves, they sometimes are overprotective or overly involved in their kids' lives, which creates a boundary issue.

Blurred Lines

Emotional bonding is an essential part of good family relations. But sometimes that bond can be too strong. Some families don't know how to love and respect each other's boundaries at the same time.

Other families don't have a bond at all and are completely distant. Either way, these are both examples of *boundary issues*. Boundaries are personal limits we set to create a healthy sense of personal space.

Everyone has different standards for boundaries, and those standards may change depending on the people we're around, or in particular circumstances. Boundaries are important because they help us establish a sense of connection with others and distance ourselves from people with whom we don't desire to connect.

According to Salvador Minuchin, a pioneer in constructing the concept of emotional boundaries, there are three categories of boundaries that families fall into: clear, rigid, and enmeshed.

Clear boundaries are a balance between respect, authority, love, and supportive guidance, such as a parent who enjoys talking with his kids about their personal lives and allows the kids to speak candidly without judgment; but at the same time clearly defines rules for the kids to follow and holds them accountable.

Families with clear boundaries allow you to be yourself but have clear standards for acceptable behavior that they won't let you cross. Clear boundaries are the boundaries a family should strive for.

Families with enmeshed boundaries don't respect personal space. The family members are always in each other's business, asking inappropriate questions, and often get offended by members who have different opinions than the rest of the family.

Sound familiar? If so, you probably belong to an enmeshed family. The problem with this type of boundary is that there are no boundaries. The family roles are blurred to the point where the kids have as much authority as the parents, and siblings get jealous of a member's boyfriends/girlfriends like a spouse would. These types of families mistake enmeshment for love or loyalty, which makes it even harder for the boundaries to become clear because they think it's disloyal to assert yourself or have your own desires and beliefs.

Lastly, we have rigid boundaries, which is basically the opposite of the enmeshment, but equally as unhealthy. Families with rigid boundaries are entirely disengaged from each other and seem as though they don't care about what's going on with each other. Rigid families are limited regarding verbal communication, are very distant, and are highly unsupportive of one another.

We are the sum of our parts. Families are interdependent units that emotionally, socially, as well as *financially* influence each other. A family's financial status can gravely affect one's mental health. That said, *poverty* is a risk factor for mental illness.

Mental illnesses associated with family problems:

- Major Depressive Disorder
- Generalized Anxiety Disorder
- Oppositional Defiant Disorder
- Borderline Personality Disorder

Poverty

"Anyone who has ever struggled with poverty knows how extremely expensive it is to be poor."

–James Baldwin

Poverty is a risk factor for virtually every mental illness: major depressive disorder, generalized anxiety disorder, schizophrenia—you name it! But is it really a surprise that poverty has a connection with mental illness? I don't know about you, but for me, some of the most stressful times of my life were when I was living in poverty, and I suspect the same could be said about almost everybody. I'm by no means suggesting that well-to-do people don't experience mental illness too, but it's a fact that there is a much higher risk for mental illness amongst lower-income folks.

Of course, there are other things besides mental health that cause or worsen poverty, like racism or limited resources, for instance. However, this section will focus on the *psychological* aspects of poverty.

Less Money, Mo' Problems...

Growing up in "the hood" or in any impoverished area, presents a unique set of experiences that can give rise to emotional problems.

Most people from the hood were raised in poverty, which increases the likelihood of experiencing trauma, prejudice, and limited access to proper healthcare, all of which are circumstances that increase the risk of acquiring a mental illness.

Society, in a sense, is conditioned to ignore poverty and all the problems that come with it, as a "survival of the fittest" mentality dominates American culture. It's no surprise that the mental health complications of poverty have been swept under the rug as well.

Poor people barely have money to survive day-to-day, much less, pay for an hour of therapy; on top of that, transportation to and from appointments, and having to pay a babysitter to watch their kids during sessions make getting treatment nearly impossible.

Statistically, Black and Latinx people are more likely than whites to be uninsured. Most people are not going to pay cash money for a therapy session—especially someone who is barely making ends meet, leaving people with a tough decision to make: pay rent or get therapy. There aren't too many people who would choose therapy over having a roof over their heads.

Poverty and insecurity go Hand-in-Hand

When I say "insecurity," I mean it more in the literal sense rather than being insecure about self-esteem—even though I could definitely see how being poor could lower someone's self-esteem. The insecurity I'm talking about refers more to the stress, anxiety, and fear poor people experience because they're vulnerable to the possibility that their financial condition will worsen.

Worrying about keeping the lights on and food on the table is emotionally draining. And having a nagging thought in the back of your mind about your car potentially breaking down at any moment is nerve-wracking! Believe me, I know; I've been there many times. If you already have anxiety issues to begin with, poverty can make them seem ten times worse, and if you don't have anxiety already, worrying about money can surely cause you to have them.

Hopelessness also is a normal feeling for those living in poverty—it's a symptom mainly associated with depression. Poverty may intensify depression, but it also can be its cause. People that are poor and depressed feel like their situation will never change. That combo can make you beat yourself up and become cynical. Hell, you don't have to be depressed to feel hopeless about living in poverty, so I could only imagine what someone who is having money trouble while suffering from a mental illness such as depression is going through.

When you're poor, and your back is against the wall, you end up doing whatever is necessary to survive—including engaging in criminal activity. Unfortunately, this style of managing hardship generally leads to incarceration or antisocial behavior (apathetic criminal misconduct).

Mental illnesses associated with poverty:

- Major Depressive Disorder
- Posttraumatic Stress Disorder
- Attention-Deficit/Hyperactivity Disorder
- Schizophrenia

Recidivism

"American prisons have become warehouses for the mentally ill."

—Bryan Stevenson

One thing we know for sure is that with poverty comes crime, and with crime, comes incarceration. What most of us don't understand is why some people are repeatedly incarcerated despite gaining little to nothing from their criminal activity.

Desperation or Illness?

A few years back, when I worked as a county jail substance abuse case manager, I noticed many of my clients were regulars. In other words, some of them would go to jail five or more times in a month! Which is more than a life's worth of incarceration for most of us. And as odd as this may sound to you and me, it's a norm in jail culture.

There's no doubt that poverty alone can lead to a life of crime. If you're poor and have no opportunity or education, how can anyone blame you for resorting to crime to make ends meet? But it seemed there was more to it than money troubles that caused those men and women I came across to repeatedly end up behind bars. You'd think, at some point, they would learn their lesson, right? They wouldn't keep doing the same stuff knowing jail was going to be the outcome, would they? Well, the truth is most of them had problems that were beyond their control—mental illnesses—including substance abuse.

What's more alarming is that I'm only considering the people who were actually diagnosed by a licensed professional. There's no telling how many mentally ill inmates there actually were, but one thing I can say beyond a shadow of a doubt is that the mentally ill ones were the most likely to *recidivate*. To recidivate means to re-offend or relapse into criminal activity.

Criminally ill....oops, I mean Mentally Ill

It's disturbing how mental illnesses are viewed as a matter of personal choice, and are criminalized, instead of being treated as a sickness that should be managed with compassion and proper care. I've seen instances where inmates start out with one-year sentences that end up being several times longer because they didn't receive adequate mental health treatment while locked up. If a man isn't in the right state of mind, it's unreasonable to expect him to behave as such. Therefore, a lot of the time, in prisons, an inmate is being punished for having an illness that he has no control over.

A large number of inmates are hooked on drugs, such as crack cocaine and heroin, and they steal and deal to supply their habit. And rarely does anyone in the legal system intervene appropriately. Once a person is addicted to a drug, it's almost impossible to quit cold turkey.

Legislators are beginning to understand the connection between addiction and recidivism now that their families are being affected by drugs, namely heroin and prescription pills. But when it was black people suffering from the same sickness, no one wanted to accept just how insidious narcotic addictions really are. But I digress, perhaps I'll save that conversation for my next book.

There are several ways mental health correlates with recidivism, but there's no real consensus amongst experts about which comes first—criminality or mental illness.

Some people within the legal system have more traditional mental illnesses that play a role in their imprisonment, like anxiety disorders, depression, or trauma-based disorders, while others have more complicated disorders that tie directly into their incarceration, like schizophrenia, antisocial personality, or oppositional defiant disorder, just to name a few.

Mass Incarceration of the Mentally Ill

Folks with mental illnesses are overrepresented in the criminal justice system. Many scholars believe that the problem is a lack of access to psychiatric services and premature discharge from treatment programs. People in the legal system that receive mental treatment rarely get the help they need to keep them out of trouble.

A schizophrenic inmate once told me he has a hard time distinguishing the chatter from his cellmates and the voices in his head. A lot of inmates with preexisting conditions get worse while they're locked up.

The mental services inmates get while incarcerated are often more of a formality to satisfy legal stipulations, instead of an honest attempt to correct their disorder, as it is for people who get treatment on the outside. I'm not saying this to put all the blame on correctional institutions, because, at the same time, many of the inmates who are offered services either don't take the treatment seriously or are resistant to change because they're attending treatment programs against their will.

Either way, when they don't get the help they need while on the inside, they eventually end up back in jail.

Regardless of what inmates do with mental health services while incarcerated, being in the legal system may be the first time most people get any sort of treatment. As a matter of fact, the correctional facilities in New York, Los Angeles, and Chicago have the three largest mental health facilities in the country. There is no reason why people can't get help before they hit the streets and start committing crimes.

To me, this says a lot. It's an indication that mental health in America is being addressed far too late, and mental health is only a concern for local and federal governments after people have become a nuisance. But *pre-incarceration* mental illness only scratches the surface as far as the connection of mental illness and the legal system is concerned.

Trouble Adjusting to Freedom

One of the lesser talked about issues people face as they return to society from prison is institutionalization, which is something most of us have seen, whether it be on TV or in real life, but not many of us understand it. Even fewer people recognize it when they see it.

Institutionalization (or institutional syndrome) is a mental symptom of people coming home from incarceration after a long sentence. Basically, it occurs when somebody has deficits in social or life skills as they attempt to reintegrate into society. Usually, we do notice a little bit of awkwardness when someone first comes home, but there's much more going on that isn't as apparent.

The part that people really don't know about is the mental effects of doing time in prison. Imagine being in a dangerous environment, where you can't trust anyone, you have to watch your back 24/7, and you can't show weakness under any circumstances. Just a day of that would be traumatic for most people—I can't even fathom having to live like that every day for several years. Then on top of that, think about what it would be like after being removed from that environment and having to learn to let your guard down again. For most ex-cons, this is a tough transition. There's no switch that can be turned on and off; it takes some real mental reconstruction to adjust to being on the outside after years of imprisonment.

Although it should be, initialization isn't necessarily a mental illness. It's just a collection of symptoms that people develop as they attempt to adjust to life on the outside. When most people think of institutionalization, they think about it in a comedic way, like on the movie *Friday After Next,* when Damon kept pushing up on Katt Williams, or they think of a homeboy from their neighborhood who has been out of jail for years but still lives by prison rules. But there is a much more serious, darker, side of prison institutionalization.

Upon returning home, many ex-cons experience depression, anxiety, PTSD, among other prison-related symptoms. It's unclear whether they develop disorders after being released or while they're on the inside. Either way, a strong case could be made for both scenarios.

On the one hand, being locked up with violent criminals, and living in chaos for years can undoubtedly lead to some complications. And on the other hand, I can see how coming home and having to basically re-start one's life could cause problems too. Many former inmates return home to nothing. They move in with their family or friends, who may not fully understand what they're going through, which causes them to feel alone or hopeless. Lack of support is a risk factor for every mental illness, especially jail-related ones like depression or PTSD. PTSD is a common disorder amongst the prison population, seeing that violence and other traumatic incidents happen regularly in jails.

Parole is also an overlooked factor. The fact that your freedom can be snatched away over a technical violation or some petty crime that doesn't warrant imprisonment can hinder your ability to reintegrate into society and ends up wearing on your emotional wellness. Imagine having to worry about several years of jail time hanging over your head. That's a hell of a way to live.

Mental illnesses associated with recidivism:

- Generalized Anxiety Disorder
- Social Anxiety Disorder
- Major Depressive Disorder
- Posttraumatic Stress Disorder
- Antisocial Personality Disorder

Trauma

"There are wounds that never show on the body that are deeper and more hurtful than anything that bleeds."

—Laurell K. Hamilton,

Aside from genetics, trauma is probably the number one contributor to psychological issues. Trauma is a key factor in most mental illnesses. It's the signature feature in *Posttraumatic Stress Disorder*. As the name implies, an individual experiences psychological stress following a traumatic situation. Depression is also known to be associated with trauma as people ruminate in despair about upsetting circumstances from their past. Many people experience anxiety in anticipation of a potentially traumatic situation as well.

What is Trauma?

Although trauma is generally defined as a deeply distressing or disturbing emotional experience, the jury is still out on what constitutes "deeply distressing or disturbing," because it could mean different things for different people. In most instances, we all can agree that witnessing death or violence is pretty disturbing. But for some, a traumatic situation might mean being put on the spot by a teacher at school. For someone else, it may result from being cheated on. While another person may be traumatized from being fired from their dream job. Have you ever heard the phrase "beauty is in the eye of the beholder"? Well, the same thing could be said for trauma because it's highly subjective. So, what's considered as trauma will vary from person-to-person.

The Body's Response to Trauma

When a person experiences trauma—whatever it may be that they deem as traumatic—adrenalin streams through their body and the emotions surrounding the traumatic incident are stored in the *amygdala*, which is basically the brain's record keeper for emotions. The amygdala stores the emotional meaning of events that occur throughout our lives.

Every time we have an experience, a record (or emotional memory) uploads into the record-keeping portion of our brain. The brain reminds us of what happened to let us know whether this was a good or a bad experience, and it's the brain's job to predict and control outcomes. This means that past experiences determine our reactions to current situations, which eventually form our thinking patterns. The brain is biased towards what it knows and will follow the path of least resistance—or at least the path that *seems* less threatening. It is the amygdala that *remembers* the feelings around each of these chosen paths.

During a traumatic incident, the amygdala activates what is called the fight-or-flight response with increased heart rate and blood pressure as well as the release of certain hormones. It provides automatic, rapid, unconscious reactions to thoughts or events. The amygdala "activates" through our five senses, whenever we experience anything that reminds us of past trauma; we can be triggered by strange things like certain sounds or smells.

For example, a person may have been bitten by a dog as a child, and the pain from the bite, which caused much fear in the individual, was stored in the amygdala. So, now, as an adult, when the person comes across a dog or a situation that reminds them of the dog that bit them, the amygdala automatically actives the fight-or-flight response to protect them from re-experiencing the traumatic situation of being bitten.

Community Violence: an agent of trauma

One of the most common and emotionally disruptive means of trauma is witnessing or directly experiencing violence. Anyone, regardless of race or socioeconomic status, can experience trauma-inducing violence; however, the ghettos of the United States have a proclivity for potentially traumatic situations. That said, it's reasonable to assume that people from these communities are more likely than the general population to experience mental illnesses like PTSD, adjustment disorder, or acute stress disorder, which are all trauma-based mental health disorders.

Community violence is so complicated that it has to be separated into three categories so that it can be addressed entirely. The first category is *victimization*, which is when a person is the target in the traumatic situation, i.e., being shot at, raped, or almost drowning. Then there's *witnessing trauma*, which is experiencing a traumatic situation happening to someone else, like seeing someone die in a car accident. Lastly, there is *vicarious exposure*, which is hearing about something traumatic, which, because of high crime rates, happens a lot in inner-city communities. Vicarious exposure can be in the form of hearing about someone being killed, robbed, or otherwise assaulted. I think most people who live in high-crime areas have had vicarious exposure at some point, as it seems impossible not to have experienced such exposure.

The closer someone is to a violent situation, the more symptoms they display. Typically, someone who was directly involved in trauma may experience more symptoms than someone who had vicarious exposure. However, the effects of trauma affect everyone differently and must not be taken lightly, regardless of the level of exposure. So, if your cousin is really shaken up by hearing about a shooting that happened a few weeks ago, don't dismiss him or her; take it seriously because even though they were not directly involved in the situation, they may still very well be traumatized.

Community violence is somewhat of a rarity in most communities. But in the inner city, because of poverty, which is seemingly a prerequisite for community violence, the incidence of traumatic situations is exponentially higher than in other communities. Yet, since in the inner city, mental health is a seldom-discussed topic, many traumatic experiences go unaddressed, which tends to lead to more problems down the road.

Community violence can have a negative influence on one's behavior. Social cognition theories suggest exposure to community violence normalizes aggressive behavior, which leads people to see violence as an effective method of problem solving, making it much more likely that they will engage in violent acts themselves, leading to a never-ending cycle of trauma. It's unfortunate how we redistribute trauma unto one another. It's as if someone has to pay for the pain we experience, and it's always someone in our community. Hurt people, hurt people. And until we mend our emotional wounds, we can't stop hurting people.

People from violent areas often compare their neighborhoods to war zones like Iraq (Chiraq), but unlike soldiers who fight overseas, there is no foreseeable end to the combat.

Those of us who live in dangerous neighborhoods may feel continually at risk of shootings, robberies, or gang activity. People in these communities constantly hear about others being victimized, which can lead to them worrying about their own safety as well as the wellbeing of their families, welcoming a variety of mental issues.

Anxiety, depression, and low self-esteem are normal reactions to trauma. Many people just bottle their traumatic experiences up and hope that they will go away. Unfortunately, this strategy for dealing with trauma rarely—if ever—works. When people bottle their experiences up, they tend to be easily triggered and engage in self-destructive activities or lash out at people who don't deserve it.

Coping with problems in the wrong ways pushes you away from emotional support, which ends up making your symptoms worse.

Trauma, in any form, can be harmful to someone's mental health, self-esteem, and general wellbeing.

Mental illnesses associated with trauma:

- Posttraumatic Stress Disorder
- Major Depressive Disorder
- Social Anxiety

Self-Esteem

"The worst loneliness is to not be comfortable with yourself."

—Mark Twain

Self-esteem is basically how much individuals like themselves or how they appraise their self-worth. In my humble opinion, self-esteem is probably the most critical psychological concept there is. Whether good or bad, self-esteem is usually the driving force behind most decisions we make in life. People with poor self-esteem do some outrageous things to receive validation from others because they don't value themselves. Individuals with high self-esteem tend to behave in more functional ways, which don't degrade themselves or others. Although closely related, self-esteem is ordinarily confused with confidence, which is entirely separate.

Confidence vs. Self-Esteem

Most of us lump confidence and self-esteem into the same category. We tend to think they are a package deal, which is untrue. A person can have high confidence and low self-esteem or vice versa. Confidence refers to a person's self-belief in their abilities in certain areas of their life. Whereas self-esteem relates to how they feel about themselves as a whole, such as their value or worth. Although confidence is usually a result of high self-esteem, some people have high confidence in some areas but low self-esteem overall.

For example, we all have seen women who wear super short skirts, apparently looking for attention from anyone who will give it. Superficially, she may seem confident, but it's possible that she is lacking self-esteem and wears revealing clothing to receive validation from others.

I'm not saying every woman who wears tight-fitting clothes has low self-esteem, a lot of women genuinely enjoy wearing revealing clothes, and who am I to judge? But this still is certainly a classic example of high confidence, low self-esteem. For many, self-esteem, whether it be high or low, begins to take form in childhood.

How Self-esteem Develops

Typically, self-esteem is based on early childhood experiences and our interpretation of those experiences. The reason most people's self-esteem is shaped in these early years is that during this time, we're young and impressionable, and do not have the knowledge to make our own judgments about the feedback we receive from society.

If a child is continuously told that they are ugly or stupid, with little or no feedback suggesting otherwise, that child will likely believe the negative feedback, which will eventually mold him into a person with low self-esteem. Likewise, someone who regularly receives positive feedback from society, and is raised in a loving and nurturing environment will probably have high self-esteem.

Although our self-esteem is not exclusively based on what people say or do to us, our environment is influential because we're social learners. Everything we know has been taught to us in one way or another, that's why it's critical to convey positive messages to children. Even when you think they aren't paying attention, they are. They're always listening, learning, and absorbing information, and most of it is subconscious. Just as we feed our kids vegetables to build strong, healthy bodies, we must also feed them positive, affirming messages to build healthy minds.

Not Worthy... or Lack of Insight?

Often when I am treating depressed clients, they talk about not being "good enough" or worthless. I have to admit, this type of thinking confuses me. Yes, to an extent, I understand how people can be led to think this way about themselves. If everywhere you turn, people are telling you you're worthless, most of us—at some point—will start to believe it.

But at the same time, I, for the life of me, can't fully understand the logic behind this way of thinking—because everyone has value. Everyone is worthy of love and respect. Chances are, if someone is making you feel that you're unworthy of love or not good enough, they don't love themselves. And if they don't even love themselves, how can they say whether or not you're worthy of love?

The Emotional Consequences of Low Self-Esteem

Self-esteem is the basis for most of the decisions we make. Many people make the best of their lives because they have high self-esteem. They value their perception of themselves more than other people's opinions, unlike those with low self-esteem. People with low self-esteem view themselves in a negative light, so they expect everyone else to see them that way too. And they have a tendency towards self-destructive habits because they don't value themselves.

I've seen plenty of people repeatedly take part in risky behaviors and expose themselves to harm or other adverse circumstances, all in the name of low self-esteem. Most people—regardless of their self-esteem level—go through a wild and irresponsible phase at one point or another in their lives, but they usually grow up—and out of these activities.

We all have done things we're not proud of—I know I have, like experimented with drugs or had the occasional bar fight back in the day. But as we aged, we got wiser and began to make more rational decisions.

Then, you have those with low self-esteem who never seem to get their act together, and consistently make bad choices that negatively affect themselves as well as loved ones. Many of my former clients who struggled with self-esteem had criminal charge after charge, baby after baby, fight after fight, and so on. And in the majority of circumstances, this never-ending cycle of destructive behavior was mainly self-inflicted, because they didn't value themselves enough to want better. The interventions I would use to help them just fell on deaf ears because they didn't believe they deserved a better life.

Poor self-esteem has a way of making one cynical. You end up seeing life through completely distorted lenses. It makes people feel like there is no point in living more purposefully. If you think you are a worthless person, why on earth would you want to stop doing drugs or selling your body? I say this sarcastically, but this is the mentality of many of those who are actively engaged in the "street life." They don't leave that life behind them because, for whatever reason, they can't get the message through their heads that they matter and, indeed, are "good enough."

On the other end of the self-esteem spectrum is overly high self-esteem. It can be just as toxic as low self-esteem.

How much self-esteem is too much?

High self-esteem is essential to having a happy life. Self-esteem is a critical aspect in just about every area of our lives. Virtually everything that we do is, in one way or another, influenced by self-esteem. We all know that low self-esteem can be problematic, but one aspect of it that's rarely talked about is the extreme associated with overly high self-esteem—the opposite end of the self-esteem spectrum. That is to say, excessively high self-esteem can cause an individual just as many problems as low self-esteem.

There are a lot of great things that you can never have too much of. Sadly, self-esteem is not one of those things. Individuals with giant egos are called *narcissists*. A narcissist is a person with a distorted self-image and a presumption of superiority without any real-world accomplishments to back it up.

A narcissist may be your self-absorbed ex, your cutthroat coworker who would do anything to advance their career, or perhaps your friend that talks to you for hours about their problems but isn't remotely interested in yours. Narcissists use people to get what they want and see no error in their ways because they think that it is their God-given right to put their needs above everyone else's. They actually believe that their needs and wants are more important than other people's are.

Narcissists reveal their feelings about themselves and others through their actions, which are often manipulative and self-centered. Despite the depth of feeling that narcissism generates, and the deep-seated insecurity it compensates for, severely narcissistic people are diagnosed with narcissistic personality disorder (NPD) and can be successfully treated by a qualified mental health professional.

Manic Ego

Mania is another mental health disorder that includes overly high self-esteem as one of its most distinct features. Manic people are known to have incredibly grandiose moods, believing that they can accomplish the most unbelievable feats, even when they have no skill or experience. They experience a surge in confidence that boosts their ego to a delusional level, as if they're on a natural high. Have you ever seen that movie *Limitless*, where after taking a special pill, the guy could accomplish any task? Well, that's what it's like for people experiencing a manic episode. Well, at least that's what they tend to think.

One client I used to see had to be admitted into a psychiatric hospital after he spent four consecutive days with no sleep while working on a masterpiece painting that he was supposed to sell to a prolific art dealer. Now, the client's behavior would not be alarming if he actually was a talented painter, and he hadn't stayed up for four whole days while working on his painting.

However, this client was not an artist and had no painting experience whatsoever. Mania is a severe sickness that causes people to be admitted into a hospital to protect themselves and others (For more info, see bipolar section).

Mental illnesses associated with self-esteem:

- Major Depressive Disorder
- Social Anxiety Disorder
- Posttraumatic Stress Disorder
- Bipolar Disorder

Social Media

"Unmoderated content consumption is as dangerous as the consumption of sewage water."

—Abhijit Naskar

Throughout my lifetime, there have been few things that I can think of that have influenced our culture as much as social media. Social media allows people to get updates on their friends, family, and even their favorite celebrities and athletes. Social media also can be a handy tool for business purposes like marketing and establishing a storefront. When used correctly, social media is a very beneficial vessel to connect people. But as with almost everything on the internet, it has its cons. Social media has a dark side that can be harmful if not used responsibly.

With the onslaught of videos of unarmed black people being gunned down by police, brutal fistfights, and unlimited "thirst trap" twerk clips, social media can do a number on our emotional wellbeing. Viewing such things on the internet can amplify our sense of helplessness in society, and could cause us to needlessly compare ourselves to others.

Social media gives virtually everyone a voice, and truthfully, some people need to be silenced. They don't need a platform to amplify their stupidity. People with low self-esteem, as well as those who belong to marginalized groups, such as racial minorities, the LGBTQ community, and disabled people, are at an increased risk of being negatively affected by harmful social media content, as they are often the intended targets of those who abuse social media.

Social Media Bravado

Over the years, social media has become a breeding ground for people who overshare their personal lives, and in many cases, fabricate a persona in an attempt to incite jealousy among their followers. I don't know which is worse, between the "money-phone" pictures, half-naked twerk videos, or the "humble-brag" posts about professional achievements. But what I do know is, more often than not, people who share these types of posts are attempting to compensate for an emotional void that is not being fulfilled in real life, so they look to fill it with social media gratification, or in layman's terms, by "clout chasing."

A lot of times, these people don't feel that they are worthy of grabbing and keeping the attention of others without the antics; therefore they desperately cling to validation from others via likes, comments, and shares because, without it, they'd feel worthless. Everyone seeks validation in one way or another. But this type of validation-seeking behavior is particularly harmful because you have to keep up an act to be validated. And when you are unable to maintain the social media persona, the very people who put you on a pedestal can tear you down from it.

Social media boasting can also be emotionally harmful to people who witness it. People look at the images that others post on social media and start to think less of themselves. I mean, who wouldn't be jealous of someone if every time you checked their page, they're vacationing on an exotic island or posting pictures of a brand-new luxury car that their husband bought them as a birthday gift, while you're at home trying to set up a payment plan with your cell phone company.

But then again, most of us don't consider that we're comparing our real life to someone else's highlight reel. Simply put, we compare our day-to-day lives (flaws and all) to the best moments of our social media friend's lives. What we don't realize is that people tend to conveniently omit from social media the fact that they recently got evicted, or that they used to fail open book tests in high school, or any other embarrassing detail that wouldn't maintain their over-exaggerated, ultra-perfect, uber-successful social media persona; they only show you the part of their lives that they want you to see.

Social Media's Mental Health Impact

I don't want to seem as if I am against social media, but social media certainly does welcome a multitude of mental health issues; depression, all types of anxiety, narcissism, and some people have been known to have trauma triggered by images and videos from social media. For some people, social media can even be addictive.

In addition to social media addiction, which could probably comprise an entire chapter of its own, *cyberbullying* is a noteworthy aspect of the harmful psychological effects of social media.

Cyberbullying

Cyberbullying is probably the most blatant example of how social media can damage mental health. Cyberbullying is an aggressive and intentional way of bullying through the use of electronics. So, no, your grandma sharing embarrassing pictures of you from elementary school when you had that Gumbee haircut is not cyberbullying. However, if Grandma intended to embarrass you, then yes, Granny is cyberbullying and must be put in check.

Cyberbullying is a tremendously broad concept. There are many ways someone can be cyberbullied. It can happen via text messages, emails, websites, and any other form of technology. So, for the sake of time, I will only touch on social media-based cyberbullying.

As social media usage has increased exponentially during the past ten years or so, the level of online comedy and creativity has also increased. That said, people are more equipped to hurl insults and make fun of people who, for whatever reason, are an easy target for cyberbullies. On average, 1 in 5 people report being a victim of cyberbullying. For some, cyberbullying may have more devastating effects than traditional bullying because of its potential to reach a wider audience through mass distribution and the anonymity technology can provide.

Don't get me wrong, in my day (which was pre-social media) bullies were cruel, but cyberbullies can be downright reckless because, in most situations, the bully doesn't have to answer to anyone because the bullying may not be detected by older, less technically savvy authority figures, such as parents, teachers, or supervisors.

Memes are a Cyberbully's Best Friend

With the addition of "memes" or pictures that contain funny, political, or general information, cyberbullying is more prevalent than ever. Memes are not always used for bullying, yet, bullies, as they do with nearly everything, find a way to use them for an opportunity to pick on people. Although it's subtle, and may not be the contemporary method of cyberbullying, memes are definitely one of the top ways people are bullied online. Memes are often the primary language people on social media use to send subliminal (and sometimes not so subliminal) incendiary messages.

Memes get spread around social media like wildfire, potentially reaching millions of people. And to make matters worse, different people can manipulate and modify the memes to make them even funnier, or depending on the meme, more hurtful—which intensifies the cyberbullying component of memes.

Anonymous Bullying

There is a common belief that bullies are cowards. I believe this to be true. I think cyberbullies are probably twice as cowardly as the regular bullies, because they hide behind their keyboards and pick on people by saying things they would probably never say face-to-face.

Many cyberbullies use fake pages. Fake pages are similar to memes, as they can be used secretly, which facilitates the creation of more ruthless content because the creator is unknown and does not have to own up to what they've said or done. The fact that the cyberbully is basically unknown makes it harder to put a stop to the bullying, which will prolong the emotional damage cyberbullying victims suffer.

Cyberbullying is often a result of deeply rooted insecurities, which the bully attempts to compensate for at someone else's expense. Bullying of any kind is usually part of a vicious cycle. A bully is often a victim of someone else's bullying, which makes it even sadder because the bully knows first-hand what it feels like to be treated in this manner.

Closely associated with bullying is *hypermasculinity*, the desire or tendency to behave—to a fault—in overly macho or aggressive ways.

Hypermasculinity

"By far, the worst thing we do to males — by making them feel they have to be hard — is that we leave them with very fragile egos. The harder a man feels compelled to be, the weaker his ego is."

–Chimamanda Ngozi Adichie

Hypermasculinity is a term used to describe the exaggeration of stereotypical male behavior, such as overemphasis on strength, toughness, aggression, and sexuality. In America—the land of guns—hypermasculinity is a problem in pretty much every community, but in the black community, hypermasculinity's influence, as well as its consequences, are amplified.

One cannot address the concept of hypermasculinity (also known as toxic masculinity) without addressing the systemic nature of such. Take hypermasculinity as it relates to black men, for example. It would be thoughtless to attribute all the violence in our community to an inherent characteristic of black men. These circumstances don't exist within a vacuum. Let me make it crystal clear: a legacy of racism and oppression is what's most responsible for the violence in the inner-cites of the United States, not a natural tendency for black people to exude toxic masculinity.

I also want to note the distinction between masculinity and hypermasculinity. Masculinity is not a bad thing by any means; it is actually necessary to counterbalance femininity and vice versa. Masculinity is essential, as it provides men and boys with an example of how to solve problems and behave in accordance with social and cultural norms. Masculinity is only a problem when it becomes excessive—which is considered hypermasculinity. Hypermasculinity is so influential in our culture that it is not just a problem for males. It has an impact on the wellbeing of women too.

Hypermasculinity is a problem for everyone—not just men

If I told you women can be hypermasculine too, you'd probably think I was crazy. Well, it's true. Women can behave in hypermasculine ways and subscribe to hypermasculine beliefs, as well. You don't have to be a man to be masculine, nor do you have to be a female to have feminine traits. For the most part, everyone has masculine and feminine traits. As a matter of fact, both are needed to maintain balance in one's life.

Men sometimes have to take on traditionally feminine roles, such as nurturing kids, or exhibiting sensitivity in certain situations, like when someone is ill or passes away. And women may need to take on traditionally masculine roles when they catch a flat tire or need to shovel snow during the winter months. But just like men, women can be excessively masculine, which is never a good thing for either gender. Have you ever seen women who like to argue and fight? Or those who continuously bash men about their financial status or their lack of physically masculine traits such as muscles, or height, as if not having these traits somehow makes one less of a man? These are prime examples of hypermasculine women. But to be fair, women aren't only affected by hypermasculinity from their own doings, but also by the excessively masculine males they interact with.

No one wants to be Captain Save-a-you know what. . .

Hypermasculine men have a hard time respecting women as people. They degrade and manipulate women to satisfy their egos, thus producing a sense of insecurity—and in some cases, mental illnesses such as depression. I've treated female clients who have been mistreated by men throughout their lives. Many of them have had so many bad experiences with men that they don't trust me as a therapist, just because I am a man.

To an extent, society has rewarded hypermasculinity. The men who have the most "game" and can have sex with the most women are often the most popular and respected. Having "hoes in different area codes" and accumulating notches on belts at the expense of the humanity of women is seen as a standard of worthiness amongst men; it's as if you aren't a man unless you devalue women.

Our performance of this outwardly displayed, deeply rooted patriarchy leads us to dehumanize women as well as LGBTQ members of our community with our words, thoughts, and actions. Our culture has embraced the western male identity, which allows us to believe that we should have a natural dominance over women that permits us to touch them whenever we want to, decide independently what sexual consent is, and punish women in whatever way we see fit. This is the hypermasculinity that drives men to be combative and resentful whenever women (or anyone for that matter) speak up about sexual harassment and rape.

Some hypermasculine folks even go as far as to blindly support famous athletes and musicians that are rapists and "woman-beaters" simply because the idea of standing up for women makes them feel emasculated. Or as hypermasculine people put it, it makes them seem "soft." And as we all know, being perceived as "soft" can cause some people to do absurd things to prove their masculinity.

Deandre Levy, of the Detroit Lions, said it best in his piece *Man Up,* on consent and sexual assault: "It's truly astounding how many awful things occur in this world because men are afraid of appearing weak." And far too often, the 'awful' things that Levy speaks of are people being afraid to seek help—or even worse—violence.

Violent Proclivities

Growing up in the inner city of Detroit, there was a well-known saying: "If you tell a man to suck your dick, you better be ready to kill or be killed" as if there is nothing in the world worse than being told to suck a dick. Those who subscribe to this notion of killing someone over semi-sexual propositions have an extremely warped sense of reality and are tremendously insecure about their sexuality.

These people are so insecure about their manhood that they cling to their masculinity and guard it with their life! Sometimes, literally. The very idea of it being taken away can cause them to defend it with deadly force. The opposite of masculinity is femininity, and anything close to it, in a hypermasculine person's mind, is to be weak. And to hypermasculine people, feeling *weak*—what they consider equivalent to feminine— is worse than death.

And to be perfectly honest, I can't blame inner-city folk for acting in hypermasculine ways. Thanks to underemployment and capitalist media outlets (i.e. rap videos and gangster films) that push a gangster agenda onto our young boys and men just to turn a profit, many young men growing up in the hood think being a "street nigga" is the only way to be a man, as the streets offer , seemingly, the only feasible opportunity for success.

What's even more troubling to me is that many black kings somehow take being called a street nigga, a thug, or a goon as a compliment.

Young brothers have such a desire to be validated as masculine, that they degrade themselves and allow others to degrade them to garner approval as a masculine being.

Violence in the ghettos of America has become so normative that its hypermasculine aspects are embraced more than condemned. Don't get me wrong. I know much of the violence in cities like Chicago or Detroit is due to social issues like segregation, drugs, poverty, and so on. Still, America's obsession with guns, and the glamorization of organized crime—at minimum—have a negative influence on violence in the black community.

Much of black youth idolizes gangsters, movie stars, and rappers who glorify street life. However, I am a huge fan of rap music—because I believe some rappers' backstories are truly amazing and motivational to people who come from similar backgrounds. I can also say with conviction that most of rap music is similar to propaganda, as it continually reinforces hypermasculine norms to black men, and even worse—black boys.

Rap is everywhere. Pretty much anywhere you go, you will hear someone playing rap music that is basically advertising the degradation and genocide of black people. Most people who listen to rap and idolize rappers don't realize that the messages in the music are damaging. How would they, when drug dealing, robbery, and murder are always being positively reinforced through rap lyrics? Most people don't want to be a drug dealer or a thug. They want the validation that comes along with that lifestyle of being tougher, and stronger, than the next man, which is hypermasculinity at its finest.

Hypermasculinity is uniquely pervasive in inner-city culture. I know it's somewhat controversial to suggest that hypermasculinity is worse in the inner-cites, and to a certain extent, it may be an erroneous claim to make because hypermasculine individuals are everywhere, not just in our neighborhoods! If you don't believe me, check out some of the bars in the Ozarks or Appalachia on a Saturday night. Or spend some time at an MMA fight or a NASCAR race. Also, corporate America reeks of hypermasculinity, as many CEOs are known for being macho bullies that demean and undercut anyone they see as weak, as they tend to endorse dog-eat-dog work environments. But even with all that being said, I'd be lying if I told you hypermasculinity in our community wasn't a significant problem too.

The socialization of men needs to change. Manliness doesn't need to be defined as unlimited strength, never showing any emotional vulnerability. It should be defined by having a range of emotions. And men, as well as young boys, should be comfortable sharing their pain and asking for the support they need.

Expanding the Range of Masculinity

Men internalize their feelings out of fear of being seen as weak. Some men hate the very fact that they have emotions in the first place. Even if they haven't outwardly expressed them! Extreme concealing of emotions –especially distressing ones—leads to dysfunction, which can be a contributor to mental illnesses.

Men have difficulty expressing themselves, and I believe most men are much more insecure than they care to admit. Culturally, it has been consistently taught to men that showing emotions is to be weak, which makes men hesitant to display any emotion except for those that project an image of strength or dominance. This is a truly toxic way of thinking because not showing or acknowledging your feelings does not mean that they aren't there. Just like anything else in life, feelings just don't go away when you ignore them: they eventually resurface and will be much more painful than they were before.

Stuffing your feelings deep down, in hopes of not being seen as weak, is called *suppression,* which is a defense mechanism people use to avoid the discomfort that comes from emotional vulnerability.

Emotional vulnerability is essential to the emotional health of men. And elevating the conversation about how men and boys are socialized to disown and reject their feelings is key to combating the high rates of suicide and substance abuse amongst black males. Also, emotional vulnerability is essential to emotional intelligence, which is a protective factor against depression and suicide. Men must know that it is okay to express their feelings, and the best way to get them to know that is to promote a cultural environment that supports and encourages men to share their pain and experiences, rather than ridicule and condemn them for seeking support.

Mental illnesses related to Hypermasculinity:

- Major Depressive Disorder
- Generalized Anxiety Disorder
- Posttraumatic Disorder
- Antisocial Personality Disorder

Common Diagnosable Mental Illnesses

In this section, I will touch on the most common mental illnesses that I've encountered in my career. When it comes to mental illnesses, the vast majority of people in general population (those who aren't mental health professionals) only know about the most prevalent disorders such as major depressive disorder, which is usually just referred to as depression; generalized anxiety disorder, normally denoted simply as anxiety; or posttraumatic stress disorder, more commonly known as PTSD. But there are many other mental disorders that are just as common that the average person needs to be made aware of, as knowledge of them may save a life.

Generalized Anxiety Disorder

"Man is not worried by real problems so much as by his imagined anxieties about real problems."

–Epictetus

Outside of major depressive disorder (which I will discuss later), generalized anxiety disorder is probably the mental illness I've seen most frequently in my career as a therapist. Most of the clients I've seen have some variation of anxiety because several mental illnesses include anxiety to some extent. But general anxiety, hence the term "generalized anxiety disorder," is the most common.

What is Generalized Anxiety Disorder?

Generalized Anxiety Disorder (GAD), often simply referred to as "anxiety", is a mental illness characterized by excessive worrying about a variety of different topics and situations. GAD goes beyond normal worrying that we all experience. GAD worrying is long lasting and intense and often happens without provocation. People with GAD tend to anticipate disaster about things such as money, health, work, and relationships. Some people with GAD know exactly what the source of their anxiety is, while others experience uneasiness and apprehension for no specific reason.

People with GAD can't shake their concerns. They often report feeling like they're taken hostage by their worries. Much of the time, they know their fears are unwarranted, but still can't move past worrying, which makes their anxiety even more frustrating. GAD can be extremely nerve-wracking because there may not even be a "worry" per se that is causing the anxiety. Yet, the individual may still experience severe physical symptoms like muscle tension, fatigue, sweating, or a lump in the throat. Also, GAD causes many people not to get much sleep—if any at all. But, for some, anxiety causes fatigue, thus an increased need for sleep. Some people dread the physical symptoms of GAD more than the psychological symptoms.

I Can't Stand This Feeling

Many studies demonstrate that people with anxiety develop *anxiety sensitivity*, which is basically a fear of the physical symptoms of anxiety.

Many GAD sufferers report fearing chest tightness, shortness of breath, and heart palpitations. People have told me they literally thought they were going to die when experiencing these symptoms because it seemed like they were having a heart attack or a stroke. Most people who develop anxiety sensitivity dread it so much that they try to avoid it at all costs, which never works.

The technical name for this phenomenon is called a *panic attack* (also known as an anxiety attack). When panic attacks occur repeatedly, or one experiences frequent worrying about potentially having a panic attack, he or she is diagnosed with panic attack disorder, which is closely related, but is a separate illness from GAD.

Is Generalized Anxiety the Same as Fear?

Anxiety is different from typical fear. Fear is a basic response to a situation, specific object, or circumstance that involves the perception of actual or perceived danger. People experience fear all the time. It's actually normal to have fear at times, like before a fistfight or during a roller coaster ride. Fear is usually a temporary feeling that is situational, or a peripheral thought in the back of our minds. Anxiety is much more insidious. Anxiety is generally based, initially, on fear, but extends into an intense preoccupation with a troubling thought that crosses the boundary of normal fear and shifts into an abnormal sense of uneasiness that is persistent and much more distressing than a temporary or situational discomfort such as fear.

Anxiety is almost always based on future events. It's driven by "what if?" thoughts. We don't get anxious about things that have already happened. Anxiety comes from the unknown and future adverse situations or catastrophes. People with anxiety get caught up in thoughts like *What if my mind goes blank during my final exam? What if I miss that important deadline at work? What if I'm not able to find someone to love me? What if something bad happens to my kids at school? What if I get sick?* The main problem in GAD is that we tend to overestimate the likelihood and intensity of danger.

Catastrophic Thinking

GAD causes people to be continuously on edge, always expecting the worse of nearly every situation. This sort of thinking is called *catastrophizing*. When anxious, we tend to catastrophize about seemingly ordinary situations; we think the worst-case scenario is much more likely to happen than it actually is. For example, having an unexpected meeting with your boss, you might think *I'll probably be told that I'm doing a terrible job. I'm going to get fired, and I'll be so anxious during the meeting my boss will probably wonder what's wrong with me.* While this worst-case scenario is certainly possible, a person with GAD disproportionately predicts this outcome and underestimates their ability to manage the situation if it were actually to happen. In other words, they overestimate the likelihood of catastrophes and underestimate their ability to cope with them.

Anxiety causes people to think in irrational ways. Most of the time, irrational thinking is used to protect us from potential danger. Because we are creatures of habit, we repeatedly do what we think works for us. Unfortunately, irrational thoughts are usually unhelpful, and eventually become a pattern of thinking, which we use to keep us "safe," or at least we think it keeps us safe.

One of the most common irrational thinking patterns used is *intolerance of uncertainty*. People who think this way tend to have negative reactions to unpredictable or uncontrollable circumstances or events. They always need to know what's next. Anxious people prefer routines and cannot tolerate even a slight bit of uncertainty.

The problem with this sort of thinking is that many things will cause uneasiness because the thoughts are future-focused, and there is no possible way to predict the future with the absolute certainty they need. One common uncertainty intolerance is about physical health. People with GAD want to be sure, without a doubt, that they won't get sick. But no one is unequivocally certain that they won't be ill at some point in their lives. Yet, most of us accept this fact and live our lives without much worry, but this is a fact of life individuals with GAD simply cannot accept, causing them to obsess unnecessarily about their health.

On the Run from Anxiety

When anxious, you experience unshakeable thoughts that can ruin your day, week, or month. Not to mention, such thoughts can destroy your personal and professional relationships. People with anxiety try to do everything possible to avoid their symptoms, ducking and dodging any and every potentially anxiety-provoking encounter, which eventually distorts their perception of danger.

Escape and avoidance are the two most common strategies used to alleviate anxiety. On the surface, it might seem like leaving the situation is the best course of action, but what it really does is confirm that our thoughts are real threats and that we are too weak to stand up to our fears and vulnerabilities. When you avoid anxiety, you're not doing yourself any favors. All you're doing is masking the problem and putting it off for another day. In actuality, the problem will worsen over time because the more you avoid anxiety, the less tolerant you are with it. One of the best ways to manage anxiety is to reduce your reliance on escape and avoidance tactics.

What are the Symptoms of Generalized Anxiety Disorder?

The most common symptoms of generalized anxiety disorder are:

Mental

- **Excessive worry**: an intrusive, continuous sense of worry
- **Restlessness:** inability to relax or enjoy oneself during leisure time
- **Loss of focus:** difficulty concentrating
- **No tolerance for the unknown**: needing to know at all times what is going to happen and how it's going to happen.
- **Expecting the worse**: a constant feeling of nervousness or dread
- **Persistent irritability:** moodiness about situations that wouldn't usually cause frustration

Behavioral

- **Escape behaviors:** escaping from anxiety-producing situations.
- **Avoidance**: Feeling overwhelmed and avoiding circumstances that cause anxiety.
- **Sleep Disturbances**: not being able to sleep because you are in a constant state of worry. Or sleeping too much because you're exhausted from worrying.
- **Jitteriness**: feeling jumpy or on edge (i.e., being easily startled)

Physical

- **Muscle pains:** aches and tightness in muscles and skin
- **Perspiration issues**: sweating and dry mouth
- **Headaches:** tension headaches (headaches that feel like a band is around your head).
- **Upset stomach:** causing nausea or vomiting
- **Trembles and shakes**: sometimes, anxiety causes noticeable shaky movements (shaking out fear).

According to the DSM-5, to be diagnosed with GAD, a person must have persistent worry about a variety of everyday situations for at least 6 months. Aside from worry, at least three of the following symptoms must be present.

- Irritability
- Muscle tension
- Difficulty concentrating
- Sleep disturbances
- Easy fatigue
- Restlessness or feeling on edge

What Causes Generalized Anxiety Disorder?

As with most mental illnesses, there is no clear-cut answer regarding the cause of GAD. It's caused by a combination of genetic, behavioral, and environmental factors. Research suggests that GAD is most likely a defect in how the emotional control center of the brain (the amygdala) processes worry and fear. Genetics also play a huge part in developing GAD. People with family members that have GAD have an increased likelihood of getting the disorder, especially in the presence of stressful life events. Also, long-term substance abuse increases the chance of GAD, as the chemicals in drugs and alcohol, as well as tobacco and caffeine, can increase anxiety levels.

Frequency of Generalized Anxiety Disorder

The Anxiety and Depression Association of America (ADA) believes 3.1% of the U.S. population has GAD, which translates to about 6.8 million people[4]. Women are twice as likely as men to be affected by the disorder. GAD symptoms can start at any age, but between childhood and middle age is when people are most at risk of acquiring GAD.

White Americans are more likely than most other ethnic groups to be diagnosed with GAD. According to a large-scale mental health study, 8.6% of White Americans will experience symptoms of generalized anxiety disorder in their lifetimes, compared to just 5.8% of Hispanics, 4.9% of Black Americans, and 2.4% of Asian Americans[5]. Although all the statistics state that white people have anxiety disorders at much higher rates than minorities, it appears the reporting numbers are much lower for minorities because, historically, minorities tend to be embarrassed about their mental health problems or they dismiss the importance of mental disorders, which leads to underreporting.

Risk Factors

There are several risk factors associated with GAD. Not having any of GAD's risk factors doesn't mean that it's impossible to have GAD, nor does having several mean that you will have GAD. Risk factors simply mean you have an increased probability of developing GAD compared to people who don't have risk factors.

Here are some of the most common risk factors for GAD:

- **Sex**: Women and girls are more likely to experience GAD due to hormonal factors and cultural expectations. They are also more willing to actually report GAD symptoms, unlike men and boys.
- **Family history**: GAD tends to run in families. This can be because of family dynamics, such as ineffective coping skills across generations, problems adjusting to a new environment, feelings of inferiority, alienation, and loss of strong family ties.
- **Genetics**: About one-fourth of first-degree and second-degree relatives will have an increased risk of GAD.
- **Substance Abuse**: Smoking cigarettes, excessive use of caffeine, and the use of drugs such as marijuana, cocaine, or alcohol can all increase one's risk of GAD.
- **Medical conditions**: people with chronic illnesses such as heart disease, cancer, or diabetes.
- **Socioeconomic factors**: People who belong to economically challenged social groups have an increased risk for GAD. This is usually due to a lack of financial security, which can foster a perpetual sense of uncertainty.

Protective Factors

- **High self-esteem**: People with high self-esteem are usually confident that bad things won't happen. At the very least, they don't expect bad things will happen, as people with GAD almost always expect the worst.
- **Internal locus of control**: People with an internal locus of control believe that they are in control of their own destiny, and can influence events and their outcomes. While those with an external locus of control believe that life just happens to them, and they have no control over their circumstances.

- **Constant physical activity**: physical activity produces endorphins—a chemical in the human body that acts as a natural painkiller, improves sleep, and reduces stress.
- **Secure attachment style**: people with secure attachment are less anxious because they have confidence that their attempts to make connections will be reciprocated.
- **Active problem solving and coping skills**: individuals with practical coping skills take action on issues that make them anxious, which will help to reduce anxiety symptoms. Those without sufficient problem-solving abilities passively wait for the anxiety to go away.

Case Example: Generalized Anxiety Disorder

Background

Meet Jada, a 30-year-old attorney. She and her husband Carlos have been married for five years and have a six-year-old son, Aaron. The family has, for the most part, always gotten along, until the *last five or six months*.

Born and raised in Atlanta, GA, Jada has lived a relatively simple life. She has a good marriage, a healthy child, and an incredible career. But for some reason, Jada is almost always on edge, expecting something terrible to happen. There's rarely a time when she isn't worrying. It doesn't matter how unimportant the situation—she will worry about it.

It's possible Jada's uneasiness began in childhood, as her parents had a rocky relationship, and their fights usually played out in front of Jada and her siblings. Her parents married young and both were immature. They couldn't handle the pressure of raising a family at such a young age, and it showed in how they handled differences. Almost every disagreement led to shouting matches or physical altercations.

Jada's parent's divorced when she was eight. She had a close relationship with both parents and felt torn between them during their drawn-out custody battle that her mom eventually won. After the split, she didn't hear much from her dad. She'd often wonder how he was doing, knowing that he lived alone; sometimes, Jada felt guilty about him having to leave the family. Four years after the divorce, her father died of cancer.

Impairment from Disorder

Although she missed her father dearly, Jada was not overly distraught about her father's passing, as she accepted his death as a part of life. But she did begin to worry about her mother's health, even though her mom has always been extraordinarily healthy.

According to her mother, Jada is overly protective, and is unrealistically worried about situations that have little to no chance of happening. Not only does she worry about her mother's health, she always urges her husband to get checked for cancer because she doesn't want him to "end up like her dad." Her husband believes that she is overprotective of their son, too, because she won't let him out of her sight, not even to spend time with his cousins who live just a few houses down the street.

Jada's anxiety is also problematic at work, as she's always on edge, unable to concentrate, and can barely sleep at night during the week. One time her boss texted her and said that he needed to talk to her later. Her mind wandered all over the place, imagining horrific scenarios. She spent the entire day speculating about what he wanted. The worrying and overall sense of uneasiness had gotten so intense she vomited, then went home for the rest of the day.

Unsurprisingly, Jada had gotten all worked up for nothing. The next morning, she met with her boss. He wanted to congratulate her on the outstanding job she'd done on closing a case with a high-profile client.

Jada's family describes her as having a nervous personality, always bothered by something. Her mother says she's a "restless soul." And because of it, she doesn't get along with most of her family. She tends to be irritable with them when something is on her mind. Her husband and son both agree she worries too much and gets mad at them for not being as worried about things as she is.

Mental Health Dx (Diagnosis)

Formal Diagnosis: Generalized Anxiety Disorder

Justification for Dx

Time period of symptoms: greater than six months

Persistent worry: worries excessively about the safety and health of her family without any legitimate reason to have a heightened level of concern about their wellbeing.

Irritability: the family says she is easily irritated when they do not have the same level of worry about situations as she does.

Sleep Disturbances: can barely sleep at night during the week.

Major Depressive Disorder

"Every man has his secret sorrows which the world knows not, and often times we call a man cold when he is only sad."

—Henry Wadsworth Longfellow

Major depressive disorder (MAD), also known as depression, is a pervasive mental disorder. Most of the symptoms of depression are seemingly normal behaviors. Often the symptoms can be easily mistaken for typical, everyday moods we all experience. For that reason, many people with this illness don't get help right away.

Though it's a severe disorder by itself, a good number of other mental illnesses include depression as a symptom. For example, Post-traumatic stress disorder includes many symptoms that overlap with depression, such as self-deprecating thoughts, irritability, and trouble sleeping. Consequently, many disorders are misdiagnosed as depression because, at first glance, a lot of them look a lot like depression.

What is Major Depressive Disorder?

Depression is a mood disorder that affects your thoughts, emotions, and even your behavior. Perhaps the most distinctive feature of depression is unshakeable sadness. This is the only extent to which most people understand depression. It's true, depression does come with great sorrow, but there's much more to it the average person doesn't even know about. In many cases, depression can dictate your appetite and sleep patterns. Some depressed people eat way more than usual, and others cannot eat at all. The same can be said for sleep patterns; some people sleep much more than they usually do, while some can't get any sleep.

Depression can put a stranglehold on your life because it affects everything you do. And one of the most troubling parts about it is that the average person who is depressed does not even know they have this condition. They just think that they are going through tough times! Not at all am I saying that a poor mood automatically means you're depressed, but depression is much more prevalent than people realize.

Depression: A Mental Illness that Flies Below the Radar

Depression is an extremely devitalizing condition; its symptoms might make you feel as if a ten-thousand-pound anchor is holding you back from living your best life, but are subtle enough not to be recognized when experienced. Because of its regularity, most of its symptoms are mistaken for normal, everyday behaviors. We all know a family member or friend who spends hours on the couch watching TV or playing videogames. Or people who appear to avoid productive activities like finding employment, socializing, or keeping up their physical appearance. At first sight, depression looks a lot like laziness. So, no wonder people respond to it with contempt and frustration instead of compassion.

Depression's symptoms usually branch off into other problems, which makes solving them seem impossible. Depressed people socially isolate themselves from others, which tends to be misread as standoffishness, thus limiting one's access to community resources and emotional support from family and friends.

Depression on the Inside and Outside

The pain from depression is not just limited to one's mind. It can be physical too. And no, I am not talking about only in rare cases either. The physical signs of depression are quite ordinary. During the evaluation period of therapy, lots of patients mention having physical sensations such as muscle pains, headaches, upset stomach, and more.

Loss of energy and motivation are also noteworthy components of depression. Living an active life with depression is no small feat. Even simple tasks like getting out of bed in the morning can seem like a monumental obstacle for people with depression. So, if you notice someone is never in the mood for anything or is always tired, there may be a good chance they are depressed.

One of the best strategies for alleviating the loss of motivation caused by depression is to be active; I know that sounds rather simple, but that's precisely what you need to do. You're probably thinking, *that's easier said than done*, which it definitely is. But sometimes, complex problems have simple answers. One of the main things I tell clients who are struggling with motivation is, sometimes you have to be like *Nike* and "just do it." Go and hang out with friends even when you're not in the mood to leave your room, or get a workout in at the gym when you're not even, in the slightest bit, up for it.

Sometimes the loss of drive that comes from depression isn't always so apparent; lethargy and social isolation aren't the only way it presents itself. Sometimes it takes the form of excessive procrastination or disinterest in things you usually enjoy. It can be as simple as a loss of fulfillment in hobbies that were once pleasurable or difficulty finding the will to clean your home.

Distorted Thinking

Researchers in the mental health field have theorized that the way we think contributes to depression. It's not necessarily the situations that happen to us, it's the way that we think about those situations that gives rise to negative emotions, which ends up leading to depression. Aaron Beck, a pioneer in psychology, believed that depression is caused by predictable, dysfunctional thinking patterns. These patterns are called *thinking errors*.

Thinking errors are negative thoughts we have without thoroughly analyzing a situation, and are based on beliefs we hold (about ourselves, others, or the world in general) without sufficient information to support them.

Anxious people catastrophize situations by thinking of the worst-case scenario, rather than the most realistic or likely scenario. This is a thinking error because a prediction of a future outcome is made based on a bias towards negativity, which has no factual basis and is only supported by a lack of confidence in oneself, others, or the world altogether. *Depressed* people do this too. They think the world is conspiring against them, and only pay attention to factors that confirm their negative thoughts.

Don't Push Me, I'm Close to the Edge. . .

Grandmaster Flash & The Furious Five's lyrics, "Don't push me, I'm close to the edge, I'm trying not to lose my head. It's like a jungle sometimes, makes me wonder how I keep from going under," always stood out to me as a call for help that is very familiar to the black community, yet that call is rarely answered. Although they were well before my generation of rap music, and certainly before my time as a therapist, I can still identify with the sentiments of these lyrics, as they are still relevant to this day for people in the inner cities across the United States. Nearly every day, I run across people on the brink of self-destruction (or the destruction of others) as they're trying to juggle poverty and keep safe in a crime-ridden environment.

Countless clients have told me how they feel like they're "close to the edge," and one more setback or misfortune would make them completely lose it. And by "lose it," I mean doing bodily harm to themselves or someone else.

Living in a ruthless environment, as some ghettos in America are, is tough for anyone, but there is added pressure for depressed people because depression causes unclear thinking. This may increase one's sensitivity towards stress—which undoubtedly increases the probability of suicidal or homicidal thoughts.

Depression is so Toxic

Not only does depression cause sadness, irritability, sleep problems, muscle tension, suicidal thoughts, and many other complications, it also completely distorts the way that you see yourself, which is probably the most challenging part of depression to manage. Depression makes you question everything, from your looks to your career choices, even your worthiness of love and respect. It can also make you question your own existence, leading you to believe that you're a useless waste of space.

Depression has a way of tricking us out of our sanity. It promotes irrational thoughts like *I'm unlovable; I'm a loser; I'm destined for failure* or some other totally erroneous self-deprecating belief. Most healthy-minded people immediately recognize these ideas as unrealistic or, at least, temporary feelings that quickly pass. But the depressed mind has a much harder time shaking these thoughts, and is easily tricked into accepting such thoughts as facts rather than mere opinions.

When in a depressive state, it's easy to slip into patterns of dysfunctional thinking. For instance, you might overly *personalize* situations. This means you think things people say or do are in reaction to you, or you believe you are responsible for things they do or say. *"He looked at his watch because I'm boring."*

Depression can make you have a *negative bias* against yourself, too. Yes, you read that right: a negative bias against yourself. Depressed people filter their thoughts to only support the negative assumptions or opinions they have about themselves, and completely ignore any positive or neutral things that contradict those negative thoughts.

What are the Symptoms of Major Depressive Disorder?

The most common symptoms of Major Depressive Disorder are:

Mental

- **Bad mood:** a persistent sad or empty mood
- **Feelings of hopelessness/helplessness:** hopelessness or feeling a loss of control
- **Self-deprecating thoughts:** guilt, worthlessness, and self-doubt
- **Irritability:** being "short" or cranky with people
- **Difficulty focusing:** problems with concentrating, remembering, or making decisions
- **Suicidal ideation:** thoughts about suicide or death in general

Behavioral

- **Lack of interest in things that used to be enjoyable:** loss of enjoyment of hobbies and activities.
- **Social isolation:** separating self from others
- **Loss of motivation:** lack of will to accomplish essential tasks
- **Sleep disturbances:** difficulty sleeping, early-morning awakening, or oversleeping

Physical

- **Energy loss:** low energy or fatigue
- **Sluggishness:** moving or talking slowly
- **Physical sickness**: headaches, cramps, muscle tension, or digestive problems (i.e., constipation/diarrhea) without a clear medical cause
- **Appetite disturbances**: changes in appetite—eating significantly more or less than usual

Not everyone who has depression experiences every one of these symptoms. Some people experience just a few, whereas others may have several. If you notice at least five of the above symptoms on more days than not, within a period lasting longer than two weeks, you might be depressed.

What Causes Major Depressive Disorder?

For some, depression is more about a low level of *serotonin* than circumstances. This fact crushes the notion that people who have everything—looks, money, and fame—don't have anything to be depressed about. Serotonin is a chemical in the human body that is responsible for a variety of functions. The main functions that relate to depression are that it is believed to help regulate mood and social behavior, appetite and digestion, sleep, memory, and sexual desire. It is known as our body's "happy chemical" because it contributes to our happiness and wellbeing.

Low serotonin is not the only thing that can cause depression, though. Environmental factors can be just as much of a factor as biological or genetic reasons. It is believed that some people are born with a tendency towards depression and that it can be activated by certain situations such as negative early childhood experiences, trauma, or some other unfortunate circumstance.

Frequency of Major Depressive Disorder

Major depressive disorder is a widespread mental illness. About 17 million people suffer from depression every year. Research implies that women are twice as likely as men to suffer from clinical depression[6]. The reason for women having such high rates of depression is unknown. It may be because men underreport their depressive symptoms, as they tend to see emotional vulnerability as a sign of weakness, which makes it unlikely that they'd admit to having symptoms at all.

Depression is one of the few psychological disorders that can lead to death. Around 60% of those who commit suicide had depression at the time of their death. But, only about 7% of men and 1% of women with lifetime histories of depression will commit suicide[7].

Personally, I think that one death because of depression is too much. Although these numbers are too high for my liking, there's a silver lining. Not everyone who is depressed will commit suicide. In fact, many get help and recover from depression.

Risk Factors

According to a Surgeon General report, African Americans are over-represented in populations that are at risk for mental illnesses—especially depression. Some of the most common risk factors are:

- **Poverty**: Low income has a strong connection to depression. Although not everyone who's depressed is living in poverty, a high number of people who are depressed happen to be poor. It's not hard to struggle emotionally when you're struggling financially.
- **Physical or other mental disorders**: Many people who have other ailments, whether physical (i.e., cancer) or another mental illness such as generalized anxiety are at high risk for depression.

- **Major life changes or stress**: Such as loss of a significant relationship, trauma, or financial problems.
- **Age**: Research has confirmed that the elderly are at higher risk for depression.
- **Insomnia or sleep problems**: Although these can be *symptoms* of depression, they also increase the risk for the disorder for people who don't already have it.

Protective Factors

Several protective factors reduce the possibility of depression, most of which involve having a support system or positive coping skills. Below are some protective factors for depression:

- **Positive family relationships**: Although people with positive family relationships can still have depression, it helps significantly to have great relationships with positive family members. Family is usually the best support system during treatment for depression.
- **Sobriety**: Alcohol and drugs act on the reward system of the brain, changing the brain's neurochemistry with continued use. Many drugs provide a surplus of happy chemicals (i.e., serotonin or dopamine) in our brain, which makes it harder for our brain to produce these chemicals naturally.

Case Example: Major Depressive Disorder

Background

Having fallen on hard times, thirty-four-year-old Jalisa moved back home to live with her mother. Jalisa doesn't know much about her father, as he left the family when she was five-years-old. Her mother and aunts are the only parental figures she's known, but she insists they were never really around because they spent most of their time partying and chasing men.

She has never been married and has three children from two different men. One of the fathers is currently incarcerated, serving a life sentence. He and Jalisa met when she was in her early twenties. The two never had a formal romantic relationship, and their interactions were mainly sexual.

Jalisa is currently in an off-and-on, long-distance relationship with James, the father of her youngest child, Armani. According to Jalisa, the couple's relationship has been mostly abusive, as James scolds and belittles her daily—and occasionally, the abuse escalates to violence.

Impairment from Disorder

Jalisa has always had bad mood spells that last for several weeks. But since moving in with her mother, the bad moods are much more intense and occur more often. Despite being unemployed and urged continuously by her mother to get a job, Jalisa has no motivation to seek employment.

Jalisa and her mom argue almost every day about Jalisa not helping with housework, as she spends most of her days sleeping or watching TV, and hardly ever leaves home. Her eating habits have changed substantially over the past few months, as well. Jalisa has been eating much more than usual—mainly sweets and microwavable meals—causing her to gain over 20 pounds.

Although her mom's criticism bothers her, Jalisa is, by far, her own worst critic, as she believes she should be more accomplished professionally at this point in her life. She also feels guilty for not being active in her child's extracurricular activities as she was before moving in with her mother. Her self-deprecating thoughts about seeing herself as a failure put her in foul moods that last for several days at a time. And the mood spells often lead to her questioning her self-worth, too, as she often thinks about all of her failed relationships, as every man she's been with throughout her life would not commit to her long-term.

Although Jalisa has thought about suicide before, she hasn't attempted or given suicide serious consideration. Nor does she have the desire or a plan to take her own life.

Mental Health Dx

Formal Diagnosis: Major Depressive Disorder

Justification for Dx

Time period of symptoms: Greater than 2 weeks

Persistent bad mood: Jalisa has recurrent mood spells that last about two weeks, but her mood spells have gotten worse and come more often since moving in with her mother.

Critical thoughts about self: Jalisa thinks harsh thoughts about herself. Yes, some of the thoughts are true, such as living with her mother, or men not wanting to commit to a long- term relationship with her, but these circumstances do not mean that she's failed at life or is unworthy of love.

Lack of motivation: Jalisa has no motivation to do anything to improve her situation. People with depression often suffer from loss of energy and motivation, which reduces the chances of them taking steps to moderate their depression. Jalisa spends most of her time watching TV and sleeping. She also does not keep up her physical appearance as she used to. At first glance, this seems like laziness, but fatigue and disinterest are two of depression's most debilitating symptoms.

Changes in appetite: Jalisa has been eating substantially more than usual. Much of which sounds like comfort food. Her inactivity, combined with her eating habits, has led her to gain 20 pounds.

Guilt: Jalisa believes she hasn't accomplished much in life and has let her children down because she is not providing for them financially or participating in their extra-curricular activities.

Thoughts of death: Although there's no plan to take her own life, she's thought about suicide as a means to end the pain.

Bipolar Disorder

> *"Some days I feel everything at once. Other days I feel nothing at all. I don't know what's worse. Drowning beneath the waves or dying from thirst."*
>
> *— The Idealist*

Bipolar disorder is probably one of the most misunderstood disorders, for people outside of the mental health field. I'm pretty sure you've heard someone call their girlfriend bipolar because one minute she's mad, and the next minute she's cool. Or you probably have called yourself bipolar because you couldn't make up your mind about whether you wanted to hang out with your friends or stay in the house on the weekend. Even though contradictory moods are a part of bipolar, that is hardly the whole meaning of the disorder.

What is Bipolar Disorder?

The disorder was once known as manic depression, but clinicians changed its name to bipolar because the term "manic depression" was too stigmatizing. Bipolar disorder is a mental illness. Let me repeat that for everyone who uses bipolar as slang: Bipolar is a MENTAL ILLNESS, not a behavior. You cannot "act" bipolar any more than you can act like you have cancer or diabetes.

Bipolar is a different type of depression that causes people to experience two entirely opposite mood disorders at once. One disorder is depression (major depressive disorder), which entails sadness, decreased energy, low motivation, and self-deprecating thoughts. The other is mania, the complete opposite: consisting of high energy, an elevated mood, abnormally high motivation, and grandiose ideas about one's self-image.

If you notice, the definition of bipolar is in its name. "Bi" stands for two disorders, and "polar," as in total opposites. Having depression alone is tough. Imagine having depression, along with its exact opposite, mania. Going through a manic episode can be like hell because sufferers experience persistent euphoric moods, overconfidence, and unlimited energy all at once. And I know, from an outsider's perspective, too much energy doesn't seem bad at all, but it actually can be extremely harmful.

Mania is no Joke

Manic symptoms can cause people to stay awake for excessively long periods with no rest, which means that their body is not getting the restoration it needs to function properly each day. This can lead to hospitalization from exhaustion. While the average person's body would probably give in after 24 to 48 hours of no sleep, people with mania don't feel tired; they just suffer the effects after the episode is over.

Mania isn't limited to staying up for long periods, it also causes people to act in an over-the-top way. They tend to have delusions of being more skillful or talented at things than they really are, and they exaggerate their importance, knowledge, and identity even though there is no evidence to support their thoughts and actions. Earlier, I mentioned a former client of mine who believed he was a world-renowned painter, even though he had never painted a day in his life before the manic episode; this type of outlandish behavior is a hallmark symptom of bipolar disorder.

Mania also causes irritability, and sometimes that irritability can mean rage, which may be dangerous depending on the person and situation. Although it's not common, manic people have committed violent acts against others as well as themselves. However, most people aren't dangerous during an episode, and the ones that are, usually have a violent background or tendency towards that type of behavior already.

Not only do people with bipolar disorder have to deal with the extreme highs from mania, but they also have powerful lows that come from the depressive aspect of bipolar disorder. Depression tends to put a strain on a person's self-esteem and motivation to do anything productive. This illness causes moods to fluctuate between high and low, but not in the rapid, stereotypical way people believe bipolar does. Most people with bipolar disorder rarely experience the manic side. Their encounters with bipolar primarily consist of depression. Depression experienced with bipolar is no different from major depressive disorder. So I won't spend much time discussing it because everything you need to know has been addressed in the depression section of the book.

There are two main types of bipolar disorders: bipolar 1 and bipolar 2. Both types are fundamentally the same, except those with bipolar 1 experience full-blown manic episodes. People around them are pretty sure something is wrong because of their outrageous behavior, while people with bipolar 2 experience a less intense version of mania called *hypomania*. Hypomania can easily go undetected because many of the indicators are more along the lines of irresponsibleness and oddness rather than the more stereotypical psychotic behaviors like full-blown mania—as seen with bipolar 1.

To clarify, during bipolar 1 manic episodes people exhibit exceptionally abnormal behaviors like running up the street naked or staying up for several days without sleep. Bipolar 2 hypomanic episodes are strange, too, but aren't as outrageous. Bipolar 2 is more along the lines of experiencing a racing mind or going on spending sprees.

These are both oversimplified examples of each type of bipolar. There's no set-in-stone way to determine which bipolar type is present without adequate training. If you suspect someone is manic, contact a mental health professional immediately.

Risky Behavior

The painting situation is a little milder than some of the things I've seen unfold behind bipolar disorder. Sometimes, people who are experiencing mania (or hypomania) do more harmful things. During manic episodes, people become more irritable, more impulsive, make reckless decisions, and take unusual risks.

One thing that I can say about my dealings with bipolar people throughout the years is that when in a manic state, it is not uncommon for them to be highly impulsive. I've witnessed families be torn apart by the actions of a family member's recklessness during manic episodes. One couple I saw for treatment was on the verge of divorce because of financial problems caused by the wife's manic shopping sprees. And I'm not talking minor spending at the dollar store. She would randomly buy flat-screen TVs, appliances, and enough groceries to feed an army. Even though she didn't do these things often, she did them often enough that she put a relatively well-to-do family on the brink of poverty.

The manic side of bipolar can cause binges beyond just spending sprees. Increased sex drive is a well-known symptom, which is nothing but trouble for married folk, as the combination of a heightened sex drive and impulsiveness may lead to promiscuity.

After manic episodes, people who've engaged in risky behavior generally feel ashamed of themselves for things they've done, because most of the time they are acting completely out of character.

Elevated Mood

With bipolar disorder, you see the worst of the worst on both ends of the mood spectrum. With bipolar depression, you are exceptionally down, sometimes not even having enough motivation to get out of bed. And with mania, you have too much motivation, to the point that your ambition is so unrealistic it could (and often does) have harmful consequences. But one thing about bipolar's elevated state that is understated is that it isn't always in the form of happiness or confidence. Sometimes, it is the very opposite—an amplified state of irritability and aggression. And those periods of elevated moods often lead to severe consequences in personal and professional relationships or with the law.

Vinny, one of my favorite clients when I worked at the jail, would come into custody like clockwork following his manic episodes. I can remember it like yesterday when he would come through booking after a long night of drinking, partying... smoking crack and shoplifting. And Vinny wasn't some street dude where this was his daily routine; Vinny was a successful businessman, but during manic episodes, Vinny went from Warren Buffet to *The Tasmanian Devil*.

Rapid Thinking

One of the most intriguing things about bipolar is the way thought processes speed up during a manic state. Manic speech is a slurred or unnaturally odd way of talking. It can sometimes be loud, fast, and hard to understand. Manic people frequently have no regard for other people's desires to participate (or not participate) in conversations; they just talk as if they're in their own world. Speech sometimes involves excessive joking and dramatic mannerisms. However, if the person's mood is irritable rather than expansive, speech may consist of complaints, hostile comments, or angry rants.

A bipolar individual's mind races during a manic episode, and their thoughts move so fast that they can't articulate them. Some people say the way their mind races is similar to trying to watch three different TV shows at the same time. When this is happening, a person may jump from one topic to another or not be able to converse in a clear and organized way:

This is called *flight of ideas*. Those suffering from flight of ideas may shift the conversation to different topics several times in a matter of minutes or seconds, making it difficult to follow what they are talking about. And no, people who change the subject during conversations aren't bipolar, flight of ideas usually happens in a very strange or unnatural way.

Symptoms of Bipolar Disorder

Symptoms and their intensity can vary. A person with bipolar disorder may have distinct manic or depressed states but may also have extended periods—sometimes years—without any symptoms.

Severe bipolar episodes of mania or depression may include psychotic symptoms such as hallucinations or delusions. Individuals with bipolar disorder who have psychotic symptoms are frequently misdiagnosed with schizophrenia and other psychotic disorders.

What are the Symptoms of Bipolar Disorder?

Here are some of the most common symptoms of bipolar disorder:

Mania

Mental

- **Inflated self-esteem**: During manic states, people experience an exaggerated sense of importance or an unrealistic sense of superiority.
- **Racing thoughts**: Many people report thinking about several different things at once, and not being able to focus on a single subject.
- **Irritability**: Individuals may be unusually snappy, vindictive, or hostile.
- **Impaired judgment and impulsiveness**: People may be prone to make thoughtless decisions and engage in behavior that is likely to have negative consequences.

Physical

- **Memory loss**: not remembering things that were done during a manic episode.
- **Sleep problems**: Many people report not being able to sleep for an extended amount of time—sometimes going without sleep for days.
- **Muscle tension**: knots in muscles and aches, pains, and soreness throughout the body.
- **Clumsiness**: being "too up" or moving too fast, dropping and tripping over things.

Behavioral

- **Excessive busyness**: increase in goal-directed activity (either socially, at work or school, or sexually), especially when this is not typical behavior.
- **Unusual talkativeness:** talking way more than usual.
- **Abnormally upbeat or wired:** bizarrely energetic or hyper.
- **Highly irritable:** moodiness and uncharacteristic aggression

Depression

- See major depressive disorder section

What Causes Bipolar Disorder?

There is not a precise cause for bipolar disorder. Scientists believe several factors contribute to its development. One of which is genetics. Most people who have the condition inherited it from a relative, like a parent, or first cousin. But the role of genetics is not absolute. Some people never develop it despite having a family history.

Another possible cause of the disorder is abnormalities in the brain. Although brain scans cannot detect bipolar, it has been noted that individuals who have the condition have defects regarding brain size and functionality.

Events like the death of a loved one, financial struggles, complicated relationships, or divorce can trigger a manic state. Stress is a potential cause and a risk factor for bipolar disorder. People with this condition are most vulnerable during challenging circumstances.

Frequency of Bipolar Disorder

The average age-of-onset of bipolar disorder is about 25, but it can occur in the teens, or more uncommonly, in childhood. The condition affects men and women equally, with about 2.6% of the U.S. population diagnosed with bipolar disorder. Nearly 83% of the cases are classified as severe[8].

There are countless undiagnosed cases of bipolar disorder. Many of these cases go undiagnosed because affected people and/or their families do not recognize the signs of this illness. They may think their bipolar loved one is just "wild and crazy" and never consider the fact they may be mentally ill.

Risk factors

Bipolar disorder's risk factors are similar to many other mental illnesses. Below are some of the known risk factors for bipolar disorder.

- **High Stress**: Stressful situations such as other health problems or work-related issues can put someone at risk.
- **Substance abuse**: People who abuse drugs or alcohol are also at risk for developing bipolar disorder. Substance use doesn't cause bipolar, but it can make mood episodes worse or rush the start of symptoms.

Protective factors

- **Compliance with medication**: Taking medication as directed can significantly reduce the effects of bipolar disorder.

- **Balanced lifestyle**: Having a consistent routine, such as a full-time job or being in a committed relationship, can help contain the symptoms of bipolar.
- **Excellent Social Support**: Having family and friends that understand the symptoms of bipolar disorder and intervene appropriately during crisis situations.
- **Appropriate Coping Strategies**: Engaging in activities such as exercise, journaling, and challenging distorted thoughts are all appropriate coping strategies to deal with bipolar disorder.

Case Example: Bipolar Disorder

Background

Meet Larry, born in a working-class, Midwestern family. His parents split when he was 11 years old. And his father passed shortly after. Larry and his mother, Janice, have a close relationship; their relationship is more like a friendship than a parent-child relationship. During Larry's childhood, family members often told Janice that she was "babying" him, and she needed to set some "ground rules." Janice felt that she used all of her strictness up with Larry's father, who seemed more like a dependent than her husband because he was bipolar and would occasionally have manic episodes. The problems that came from Larry Sr.'s illness were the main reason for their divorce.

Impairment from Disorder

Larry was an average student in high school and played on the football team during his junior and senior years. He had a lot of friends in school but wasn't popular. Many of his peers thought of him as moody.

Sometimes, Larry would seclude himself. At home, he barely came out of his room for extended periods.

Larry's mother never acknowledged that he could have been mentally ill, she believed it was just teenage hormones, seeing as there were days when Larry would be over-the-top and energetic as if he had drunk 10 cups of coffee, which was opposite to the lethargic, sulky way he usually was.

Because of poor grades and disciplinary issues, Larry, a high-school football star, got zero offers from colleges to play football. So, he joined the Marine Corps as a mechanic.

Larry signed up and shipped off to boot camp without even informing anyone of his decision. No one knew he had joined the military until several months later; he was unpredictable and lacked discipline. You'd think the military would've changed that. It didn't.

He once showed up to a meeting with his superior officer while he was high, reeking of marijuana and alcohol. Throughout his time in the service, Larry had several disciplinary issues related to substance abuse. His superiors believed he had a drug problem. Yet, he rarely ever drank or smoked. But when he did, he'd go on binges that lasted for days at a time, doing reckless things that were totally out of his character.

Eventually, the marines got tired of Larry's antics and forced him out of the military. After leaving the Marine Corps, Larry spent about a year in a small town close to where he had been stationed; he bounced from home to home, mainly sleeping on the couches of friends and women he was dating.

During this time, Larry impregnated two women —whom he barely knew—within a span of 6 months. Also, during this post-military period, he racked up several criminal charges, including DUI's, domestic violence, and possession of cocaine.

Several years later, Larry returned home to live with his mother, spending most of his time in his room (the basement), isolated from the rest of the family. His family reports that he's very unpredictable. At times, he's lazy and moody. But, occasionally, for several days at a time, he's hyperactive—talking a-mile-minute, sleeping very little, and even a bit confrontational with family members.

Mental Health Dx

Formal Diagnosis: Bipolar 2 disorder

Justification for Dx

Depression: Larry displayed several depressive symptoms, such as moodiness, isolating himself from friends, and a lack of motivation (described by family as laziness).

Impulsiveness: Larry impulsively left to join the marines without telling anyone. He also impregnated many women, whom he barely knew, in a short period.

Risky behavior: Larry abused alcohol and marijuana during manic episodes. Larry went on short crime sprees that led to many run-ins with the law.

Absence of manic episode: Larry experienced hypomania (not mania, which is related to bipolar 1). It's typical for hypomanic people to do thoughtless, irrational, and uncharacteristically irresponsible things, but not necessarily be a danger to themselves or others.

Manic people, on the other hand, have to be hospitalized because they are so unstable they pose a threat to themselves and others. A person refusing to eat or sleep, having delusions, suicidal ideations, or any other behavior that is reasonably considered unsafe, warrants hospitalization.

Social Anxiety

"No one can make you feel inferior without your consent."

—Eleanor Roosevelt

Ahh...social anxiety ... one of those disorders that can easily fly below the radar because it's often mistaken as plain ole shyness. Social anxiety has a way of ruining personal and professional relationships and hampering the chances of you doing things that consist of socializing—which is basically everything. Social anxiety is a particular kind of anxiety that differs from generalized anxiety in that its basis primarily revolves around social interactions, unlike generalized anxiety, which is much broader and nonspecific.

What is Social Anxiety?

Social anxiety (SA) is an unnatural fear of situations that involve social interactions. It could be said that it's a fear of being judged negatively by others. For most people with SA, it occurs when meeting new people, going to a job interview, answering a question in class, talking to a cashier at a store, or being around unfamiliar people. Some people's SA is much worse, to the point that doing things that are ordinary to you and me may cause them severe discomfort or fear. Eating in front of others or using a public restroom can evoke intense fear of being humiliated, judged, or rejected.

The fear that people with SA have is so intense that it seems uncontrollable. They frequently believe they'll be humiliated in social situations even when it's doubtful that would happen. They feel anxiety about the very thought of being embarrassed—even when the situation has minimal significance. SA interferes with nearly all areas of their lives. Social anxiety can cause them to feel like they are walking on eggshells, just hoping something doesn't happen that causes them to be put on the spot. Being the center of attention is horrific for many SA sufferers. Fear of being the focal point is often the reason they don't take certain jobs, or ask people out on dates. Some people avoid the very things in life that would make them happy because the anxiety that comes with such interaction is too unbearable.

SA isn't always tangible. Sometimes it's just a general sense of uneasiness in social situations. Some people might feel uncomfortable but can't quite put their finger on the cause. Then again, some people can pinpoint the exact source of their anxiety, but they don't know *why* it makes them uneasy. Others understand the root of their anxiety, yet are still unable to shake the uncomfortable feelings. People experience SA in a variety of ways. There is no specific manner in which a person experiences SA. The only concrete thing about SA is that the discomfort involves social interaction.

Is Social Anxiety Different From Shyness?

Social anxiety and shyness have many similarities, but what distinguishes the two is the severity, level of avoidance, and intensity of impairment with daily activities they cause. With shyness, a person may be bashful about doing things but can quickly get over those feelings, depending on the situation. He or she might be nervous before giving a speech or asking someone out on a date but can still accomplish the task in question without a significant amount of discomfort. Whereas in the same predicament, someone with SA would worry for days, weeks, or even months beforehand, probably losing sleep, and then obsessing after the fact. They would say to themselves, *He probably thinks I'm an idiot,* or *I hope I don't embarrass myself.* Sometimes people with SA know their anxiety is irrational, yet they still worry about rejection or embarrassment.

The main difference between SA and shyness is that shyness is a personality trait that doesn't really cause much impairment in someone's life. Social anxiety is a mental illness that causes significant distress during seemingly ordinary social encounters.

Man Up

Many people think that SA is a characteristic of the weak. Like other mental disorders, the underlying thoughts behind the stigma are based on ignorance. Just as anyone can develop depression, anxiety, or PTSD, anyone can have SA. The general public tends to think SA only affects the weak. That is not true at all. A person can be tough as hell and still suffer from it. SA is a mental illness, not a personality flaw—and definitely not a sign of weakness.

Stigma and stereotypes are the main reason many people—especially men—don't seek help for the disorder. They're afraid that they'll be seen as weak—which is a catch 22. How can you ask for help with an illness you're ashamed to admit you have? Seeing that SA is an illness predicated on a fear of negative judgment, it's probable that many people suffer from it in silence.

Not seeking help is a form of avoidance. On the surface, evading anxiety may seem helpful. A person might think, *If I stay away from things that make me anxious, I'll be okay.* This type of thinking actually masks the problem by putting it on hold for another day. Sort of like using a Band-Aid on a wound that requires stitches.

Primal Instincts Meets Socialization

As with all forms of anxiety, SA affects our brain's fight-or-flight mechanism, which is designed to protect us from *real* danger—like an armed attacker or a wild animal. However, with SA, our natural survival instincts kick in at inappropriate times, causing us to misinterpret threats, which leads us to see danger in situations that aren't dangerous at all.

Our mind's functions are entirely primal. The brain is designed to protect us. So, when it's embarrassment that we view as danger, the mind doesn't discriminate, it acts in the way that it's designed to, activating all of our essential bodily functions needed to survive, such as increased heart rate, required for rapid action in the face of danger. The bad part about the fight-or-flight response is that it shuts down the bodily functions that are non-essential to survival, like our ability to reason, which is why we have a hard time not being anxious even when we know the worry is illogical.

Irrational Anxiety in Spite of Logical Thoughts

Earlier, I touched on times when people know, intellectually, their anxiety is absurd, yet are unable to eliminate the unpleasant feelings that come along with anxiety-provoking occurrences. Often, we believe the reason people have SA is that they don't know their fear is irrational. Yes, for some, this is true, but most people are aware their anxiety is illogical. For many people, simply knowing their anxious thoughts are unfounded isn't enough to alleviate worrying.

If all you needed to know was that it is unlikely the girl you want to ask on a date won't humiliate you for talking to her, or that no one is going to laugh when you speak up in meetings at work, then SA wouldn't be a problem for anyone, because usually we already know these things.

The disconnect between what we know and how we feel is rooted in the way our brains are set up to protect us from what we perceive as threatening. Thus, preventing us from moving forward even when we know—on an intellectual level—our anxiety is irrational. To change the way your mind responds to anxiety, you have to challenge its responses to supposed danger. This can be accomplished through the use of *Socratic questioning* and *behavioral experiments.*

Socratic questions are named after the legendary philosopher Socrates because the questions are deep—like the questions Socrates asks—helping you think of balanced and realistic responses to situations that cause anxiety. An example of a Socratic question is, *what evidence supports this idea?* Or *what is the worse that could happen if that thought were true?* These questions help your brain thoroughly analyze the level of threat the situation brings, which, in turn, recalibrates your fight-or-flight response to function in a more suitable way.

Behavioral experiments are also helpful regarding challenging irrational thoughts. As with Socratic questioning, the point is to test the validity of your anxiety. The only difference is that Socratic questions are questions you ask yourself about particular situations, and behavior experiments are done in real-time. For example, instead of asking *what's the worst that could happen?* With a behavior experiment, you'd actually put yourself in the situation and *see* what happens. So if your fear is answering questions in class, you'd answer a question to see if it's as bad as you believed it would be.

What are the Symptoms of Social Anxiety Disorder?

The most common symptoms of social anxiety disorder are:

Mental

- **Self-consciousness:** feeling embarrassed or awkward around other people.
- **Negative bias**: a tendency to disregard one's own personal charm and magnify the social skills of others.
- **Negative beliefs:** firmly held beliefs that you're socially inferior (i.e., I'm lame, I'm weird, or I'm too boring for someone to like me).
- **Negative thoughts**: thinking that you are somehow going to do something that will cause humiliation or rejection from others. For example, thinking, *what if everyone notices I'm nervous?* Or *what if I say something dumb?*

Behavioral

- **Avoidance**: avoiding situations or engaging in activities that may cause anxiety
- **Safety Behaviors:** taking precautions to minimize the effect of anxiety, such as rehearsing what you're going to say before a

phone call or not wearing (or doing) things that may cause you to be the center of attention.

- **Escape**: leaving situations that cause anxiety. This is different from avoidance because, with avoidance, an individual evades unease altogether. While with escape, they may not necessarily avoid unease but will leave if the situation causes too much discomfort.

Physical

- Blushing
- Sweating
- Skin turning red or flush
- Using the bathroom excessively
- Lump in throat
- Ringing in ears
- Dizziness, nausea, or blurred vision

Although many of these physical symptoms are related to SA, they are not required for a diagnosis of the disorder.

What Causes Social Anxiety?

Social anxiety can run in families. Researchers believe the cause is genetics. They claim that defects in the brain make people susceptible to SA. Others believe the reason for it is situational. Misreading the behaviors of others can play a big part in the development of SA. Thinking that people are staring at you or frowning when they are not, is a perfect example of misreading people.

Underdeveloped social skills are another likely cause of SA. If you have poor social skills, you may feel discouraged after talking with people and may worry about communicating with people in the future.

Negative beliefs about one's self are also contributors to the disorder. Many people believe that other people see the negative things that they see in themselves. And because of their negative beliefs about themselves, they expect judgment and ridicule.

Frequency of Social Anxiety

Social anxiety is the fourth most common mental health condition[9]. About 1 in 8 people have suffered from social anxiety disorder at some point in their lives. This is called *lifetime prevalence.* Any given year, about 7 out of 100 people suffer from the condition. This is called *12-month prevalence.*

The 12-month and lifetime prevalence helps give a realistic depiction of how many people are affected by the disorder. But as with every disorder, we can expect that its prevalence is substantially higher than the numbers indicate because many people underreport or don't know that they have the illness.

White Americans report social anxiety much more than people of other races. Blacks have the lowest rate of social anxiety[10]. However, those that do report the disorder are highly impaired. SA appears to have a significant impact on many marginalized populations. Handicapped people, LGBTQ people, as well as women, seem to have a high rate of SA. Young people are also vulnerable to SA. The average start age for SA is around nine to twelve years old.

Risk Factors

Countless factors can cause social anxiety, below are some of the most common risk factors:

Parenting: Parenting traits such as over-control, lack of warmth or rejection, and overprotection are known to be associated with the development of this disorder. Also, specific rearing tactics put people at risk—such as shaming, criticism, and isolation.

Toxic Relationships with Siblings: Some people use siblings as the standard to which they judge themselves. Having a sibling who is praised by others more than you are is a risk factor for SA.

Bullying: Severe and traumatic bullying is a good predictor of future anxiety problems, especially social anxiety, given the social nature of the disorder.

Gender: Evidence has long supported higher prevalence rates of SAD in females versus males.

Shyness: Temperamental dispositions, such as shyness along with environmental factors, can lead to SA.

Protective Factors

Strong Family Relationships: Emotional closeness and contact with family can protect against SA.

Engagement with Peers: Regular engagement with peers in childhood is linked to lower social anxiety, thus being involved in social activities with others may serve as a protective factor.

Attachment Security: Secure attachment patterns are believed to help prevent the development of SA. People with a secure attachment style are generally confident they will not be rejected by others, which is one of the main areas of concern for people with SA.

Case Example: Social Anxiety Disorder

Background

Born and raised in the Englewood section of Chicago, Rio comes from a working-class family. His parents worked multiple blue-collar jobs to make ends meet. He was one of very few—if not the only one—in his neighborhood to live in a two-parent home.

His father, although a hard worker, struggled with crack cocaine and alcohol addiction throughout Rio's childhood. Rio's parents were almost always at odds with one another. They would bicker and fight nearly every day.

Growing up, Rio didn't have a positive relationship with his family, as they were very critical of him because of his poor grades and seemingly moody and aloof attitude. Rio's parent's wanted him to be more like his older brother, Brian, and they often compared the two. Brian was Rio's total opposite: social, articulate, and overachieving.

Impairment from Disorder

During his middle-school years, Rio was teased by his peers for being too dark and for wearing "hand-me-down" clothes. Although he had a variety of friends in school, Rio always gravitated to the unpopular kids. On the outside, he appeared to be indifferent, but the scrutiny from his peers caused him to fear being noticed by others. Rio's discomfort with school led him to frequently skip school, just to avoid the social interaction that came along with it. Rio felt much more at ease when he was skipping school, even though deep down, he felt guilty for not going.

As he got older, into his early and mid-twenties, Rio appeared to be more confident as he started socializing more by attending parties and clubs. When under the influence of alcohol, Rio is very social and uninhibited, but without it, he is self-conscious and guarded.

Rio's social discomfort extends to his work life, as well. He thinks his co-workers and boss are always judging him about the quality of his work, despite no one saying anything about it. Sometimes Rio gets anxious because he thinks people are noticing his nervousness, which causes even more nervousness. And when he makes mistakes, he stresses about them for hours, sometimes even days, and believes that his coworkers think he is an idiot.

Pretty much anytime Rio is around people he isn't familiar with, for instance, group settings, or situations where it's required for him to speak up, he is crippled by a deep fear of judgment, embarrassment, or inadequacy. Rio's anxiety is so intense that, at times, he notices physical sensations. The muscles in his face and neck get tense, he sweats, and sometimes has even gotten headaches.

Mental Health Dx

Formal Diagnosis: Social Anxiety Disorder

Justification for Dx

Time period of symptoms: greater than 6 months.

Fear of being judged: Rio fears that his co-workers will scrutinize his work, despite having no legitimate reason to believe so.

Negative thoughts about self: Rio thinks negatively about himself in social situations. He worries endlessly about being thought of as an "idiot."

Physical symptoms: Rio has headaches, muscle tension, and sweating when anxious.

Substance Abuse: Rio uses alcohol to reduce nervousness in social situations.

Avoidance: Rio regularly cut classes in school to manage his discomfort at school.

Oppositional Defiant Disorder

"Having a mental disorder isn't easy, and it's even harder when people assume you can just get over it."

—Unknown

Oppositional Defiant Disorder (ODD) puts a strain on relationships. I say this because many of its symptoms have to do with communication and other interpersonal problems. Have you ever met someone who was disrespectful, spiteful, and argumentative all the time, for no apparent reason? Well, in a nutshell, that's precisely what ODD is. It's all-out vindictiveness, and, as the disorder's name implies, oppositional defiance towards authority.

As a youth case manager, many of the clients I dealt with were diagnosed with ODD, and just from getting the brunt of their spite, I can say that ODD is a very tough disorder to treat because ODD clients are usually resistant to following treatment plans—big shocker, right?

What is Oppositional Defiant Disorder?

ODD is a childhood condition characterized by argumentativeness, spite, and general unwillingness to conform to rules set by authority figures. The symptoms can occur in any setting, but are usually exhibited in places like school or at home. Most people who have spent a decent amount of time with an ODD child don't have many positive things to say about them, as they can be incredibly hard to get along with.

Some of the most challenging cases I've seen have been with ODD kids. Almost everything you say to them is responded to with a "smart" comeback. It is nearly impossible to have civilized conversations with them. I could tell them the sky is blue, point up to the sky to prove my point, and they will still try to find some way to disagree with me.

ODD symptoms are almost always present where the individual is most comfortable. Kids with this disorder are usually more defiant with people they know well. Thus, the symptoms don't really present themselves during the evaluation phase of therapy. It's typical for a child to gradually become more defiant as treatment progresses.

Children with ODD are the type of kids that don't get along with other children, as they intentionally do things to annoy or disrupt. Many ODD kids are labeled as bullies or outcasts because of the confrontational nature of this condition. They tend to refuse to follow instructions and often antagonize others just to get a reaction.

Although ODD is seen in many bullies, the symptoms rarely manifest into violence. ODD is primarily about stubbornness and negativity, by way of verbal aggression rather than physical behaviors.

Limit Testing

One of the most characteristic traits of ODD is *limit testing*. Limit testing is trying to see how long you can push someone's buttons before they react. Or deliberately breaking boundaries just for the sake of rule-breaking. Make no mistake, all kids limit test from time to time, but limit testing crosses into ODD territory when it becomes excessive, and is a frequent pattern, even in the face of consequences and redirection.

Many teachers have experiences with ODD children who are highly disruptive in class. They cannot be moderated, no matter what the teacher does. The disruption itself is not the basis of ODD in that situation. There are all sorts of reasons for a child to be disruptive at school. However, if the student is disruptive just to spite the teacher, that would probably be a good indicator of ODD.

Passing Blame

The peculiar thing about ODD is that regardless of how argumentative, petty, and downright obnoxious they are, individuals with ODD, hardly ever see the error in their ways. Most of the time, they blame everyone else for their actions, even when it's clear that they are at fault. Few ODD children actually believe they're disobedient. They usually think their defiance is warranted.

Unreasonable Resentment

ODD is primarily rebellion stemming from unaddressed grief. Resentment is usually the underlying factor behind the defiance. Often, ODD children project negative feelings from their past experiences onto undeserving targets.

Many *defense mechanisms* are at play with ODD, namely displacement. Displacement is when people are angry at something unfair that happened to them, but take their frustration out on people who have nothing to do with the initial situation. This is not to say their bitterness is always unreasonable, though. Some ODD children come from rough backgrounds and have been legitimately mistreated by authority figures like their parents, teachers, or foster home caretakers.

Though ODD symptoms can be troublesome, we must exercise compassion when dealing with this disorder because it is a mental illness, not a personality defect.

What are the most common symptoms of Oppositional Defiant Disorder?

Not everyone with ODD will behave the same way, but here are some of the classic symptoms associated with the disorder:

Mental

- **Quick-tempered**: frequently frustrated
- **Lack of concentration:** difficulty staying focused
- **"Smart-mouthed:"** failure to think before speaking
- **Spitefulness:** often angry and resentful
- **Moodiness:** very touchy or easily annoyed by others.

Behavioral

- **Aggression:** seemingly unprovoked blatant hostility towards others.
- **Rebelliousness:** flagrant and repeated disobedience.
- **Antagonism:** deliberately annoys people (i.e., peers, teachers, parents).
- **Severed relationships:** willingly destroys friendships and other relationships.
- **Lack of accountability:** blames others for their own personal problems.
- **Stubbornness:** unwilling to negotiate or compromise.

Physical

There aren't any noteworthy physical symptoms of ODD. It is primarily an interpersonal disorder that affects relationships rather than individual functioning, as most mental illnesses do.

What Causes Oppositional Defiant Disorder

There is no clear-cut cause of ODD. Most experts concede that the condition is a combination of biological and environmental influences along with social risk factors. There are two leading theories about the development of ODD. One theory suggests that children develop ODD because they have failed to meet certain emotional development milestones during their toddler years.

The other theory proposes that the negativistic attitudes of ODD are learned from negative reinforcement techniques by parents and other authority figures. The use of negative reinforcement by parents is believed to increase the rate and intensity of oppositional behaviors in the child as parents project their insecurities and other negative character traits unto their children. Parents that are overtly punitive, rather than constructive in their child-rearing strategies, tend to foster a general sense of resentment towards authority in ODD children—which they end up projecting on the people they encounter.

Frequency of Oppositional Defiant Disorder

ODD is one of the most common behavioral disorders in children. It is estimated that about 10 percent of all children will develop ODD. It is believed that before the start of puberty, ODD is more prevalent in boys than it is in girls. However, once puberty has been reached and surpassed, the number between the sexes becomes more equal, with the condition being said to occur in about 11% of boys and 9% in girls. Girls, however, are likely to display ODD symptoms differently than boys will[11].

The good news about ODD is that about two-thirds of those diagnosed will overcome most of their symptoms as they get older. Some studies have shown that by the age of 18, nearly 70% of children previously struggling with ODD no longer have symptoms of the disorder[12].

Risk Factors

Here are some risk factors for ODD:

- **Parental mental illness:** Studies suggest that mentally ill parents may be more likely to have children with oppositional or noncompliant behaviors.
- **Parental substance abuse:** Having a parent who abuses drugs or alcohol increases the chances of developing ODD.
- **Inconsistent discipline**: Parents who are inconsistent in their parenting (i.e., not always enforcing rules) put their children at risk.
- **Instability in the family**: Experiences such as divorce, multiple moves, and changing schools frequently create risk.
- **A history of abuse or neglect:** Children who have a history of neglect, physical, sexual, or emotional abuse are at risk.

Protective Factors

Early intervention: Studies show that early intervention and treatment will help a child overcome ODD. Treatment also may prevent its progression into a more serious mental health concern.

Attending pre-school: The Head Start program has been shown to help children do well in school and prevent delinquency later in life. Children in this program learn social skills, how to problem-solve and manage difficult emotions.

Positive parental influences: Parents who are fair and productive in their parental strategies help reduce the chance of their children developing ODD.

Case Example: Oppositional Defiant Disorder

Background

Thirteen-year-old Crystal has always had difficulty getting along with people—especially authority figures. Currently living with her parents and her 17-year-old brother, Randy, their living situation is anything but pleasant. Crystal's parents not only fight with each other nearly every day, but they also argue with her and her older brother too. The atmosphere in their household is chaotic. Crystal's brother and her father (who is not Randy's biological father) have been in multiple physical altercations because her father claims Randy is disrespectful. After their last fight, Crystal's parents put Randy out of their home.

Impairment from Disorder

Crystal has poor grades and bad relationships with her teachers and other school staff. Nearly every person at her school describes her as a troublemaker. Chrystal intentionally does things to annoy people at her school. Numerous classmates have reported incidents where Crystal has kicked the back of their seats just to get a rise out of them or repeatedly disrupted the class for no apparent reason. Some of her classmates have even said they feel sorry for the teachers who have to deal with her.

Despite countless redirections from school staff, suspensions, detentions, and other forms of punishment, Chrystal's behavior doesn't change in the slightest bit. Trying to reprimand her is like fanning the flames, as trying to correct her poor behavior usually leads to spite.

Crystal's argumentativeness and vindictiveness in school prevent her from making friends with her peers, which causes her to feel isolated and to assume that people don't like her—even before they've gotten the chance to dislike her—which seems to be a recurrent self-fulling prophecy in her life.

At home, things are not much better. Chrystal doesn't follow any of her parent's rules without first putting up a fight. Requests to do chores are usually met with hostility and anger. Chrystal's parents report feeling like they are walking on eggshells because she will lose her temper and say hurtful things to them. She also never takes responsibility for her actions and blames her family for making her have a bad attitude rather than owning her role in the situation.

Mental Health Dx

Formal Diagnosis: Oppositional Defiant Disorder

Justification for Dx

Time period of symptoms: Greater than six months.

Argumentive with authority figures: Crystal argues with parents when asked to do chores.

Refusal to follow rules: Constant redirection and corrective actions have no effect on Chrystal's disruptive behavior in school.

Deliberately annoys others: Crystal kicks the backs of other students' chairs intentionally, attempting to annoy them.

Blames others for misbehavior: Crystal blames others for causing her to have a bad attitude, rather than accept responsibility for her own actions.

Antisocial Personality Disorder and Conduct Disorder

"Some people steal to stay alive, and some steal to feel alive. Simple as that."

—V.E. Schwab

Antisocial personality disorder (APD) is one of the most culturally misunderstood mental illnesses. Just as it is with bipolar, you hear people talk about it in regular conversation. "Oh, you ain't gone speak? You're so antisocial!" This is the common contextual usage of antisocial, which is far from what the word actually means. Antisocial is nothing like it sounds. What it sounds like is someone who is standoffish or shy. But it's actually a personality disorder. Its main features consist of behavioral patterns that violate the rights of others. Simply put, it involves a deficiency in one's conscience, where they lack empathy or have a complete disregard for the human rights of others.

Children are not diagnosed with antisocial disorder—they are diagnosed with *conduct disorder*, which is more or less an abbreviated version of APD. That is to say, conduct disorder is basically the childhood version of APD. As a matter of fact, a childhood diagnosis (or

126

symptoms similar) of conduct disorder is required for an adult to be diagnosed with APD by a mental health professional.

What is Antisocial Personality Disorder?

APD is a disorder in which its sufferers don't have a moral compass. Or, at least, they don't have a functioning compass in the way that most of society does. APD is sometimes referred to as *sociopathy*. People with this disorder tend to antagonize and treat others harshly. To make matters worse, they are usually indifferent to the pain and suffering they've caused, as well as the consequences of their actions. The sad reality of this disorder is that most of the time, people with it become career criminals. This is most likely because, with the features of this condition, they cannot adequately fulfill the responsibilities of family life, work, or school.

Folks with APD lie, steal, bully others, have substance abuse issues —and can even be dangerous. But, not all members of the APD population are violent. Most of them just do otherwise morally corrupt things that aren't necessarily dangerous. However, most people who are, indeed, violent probably suffer from APD because the average person only resorts to violence in self-defense; those with APD typically initiate fights or find themselves in situations where conflicts are likely.

Of course, we all probably have started a fight or two (or three) in our lives, but antisocial people have a consistent, lifelong pattern of engaging in this type of behavior.. So, just because you had a few scuffles in grade school or have a criminal past doesn't automatically make you antisocial.

Disregard for Society's Laws

Most of us have done things we're ashamed of—which is a normal part of life. No one is exempt from regrettable behavior. I can look back at several points in my own life where I cringe at the foolish things I've done. Some of my actions were criminal, some were due to a lapse of judgment, and others were simply based on unfortunate circumstances. But the fact that I *can* look back and know I was wrong shows I have sufficient morality. That isn't the case for those with APD.

Individuals with APD lack remorse for their misbehavior. They often rationalize their wrongdoings. Sometimes they flat-out don't care about what they've done to others or how it affected them, and are entirely devoid of the ability to sympathize.

Antisocial, Sociopath, and Psychopath

Like the word "antisocial," the terms sociopath and psychopath are often casually thrown around too. But few actually know what they mean. Some people do coincidentally use these words in the right context but are mostly using them as an insult without a detailed understanding of what an antisocial, sociopathic, or psychopathic person's behaviors are.

Antisocial and sociopath, more or less, mean the same thing, and generally are used interchangeably. As we know, antisocial people have an extraordinarily limited conscience compared to those without APD.

Psychopathology is an intensified version of antisocial disorder. Psychopaths have less compassion than sociopaths, and are almost always dangerous. A sociopath would feel no guilt about hurting a stranger, but they might feel guilty about hurting someone with whom they had a bond. Sociopaths can be reformed. Their behavior may lessen over time, while this cannot be said about psychopaths. Psychopaths don't have any concern whatsoever about who they harm, the consequences of their behavior, nor do they have remorse for their actions.

Is Antisocial the same as being a Criminal?

Yes and no. Yes, because APD and criminal behavior go hand-in-hand. No, because not every antisocial person is necessarily a criminal. Sometimes, their antisocial behavior is more along the lines of being a horrible husband or wife or an otherwise corrupt individual. The main underlying factor of antisocial personality disorder is a disregard for right and wrong. It doesn't always have to be as serious as crime; sometimes people with APD just treat others very poorly.

What are the Symptoms of Antisocial Personality Disorder/ Conduct Disorder?

Common symptoms of APD/Conduct disorder include, but are not limited to:

Mental

- **Lack of remorse:** Person does not show any regret for their wrongdoings.
- **Conduct disorder:** A childhood diagnosis, or signs of antisocial behavior during childhood, is needed for a formal diagnosis of APD.
- **Irritability:** People with APD are known to be easily angered.

Behavioral

- **Disregard for Society's Laws:** Person is not following established rules despite redirection or severe consequences.
- **Violation of the physical or emotional rights of others:** Person engages in robbing, hitting, raping, manipulating, or inflicting any otherwise intentionally harmful behavior onto others.
- **Lack of stability in employment or home life:** Person has difficulty keeping a job or maintaining positive relationships with family and friends.

Physical

There aren't any physical symptoms of APD, as it is mainly a disorder that is based on personality rather than emotional or somatic distress. And because physical suffering isn't a central feature of APD, there are no noteworthy physical symptoms.

What Causes Antisocial Personality Disorder?

There are many causes of APD. Most of them are either based on biological or environmental factors. Seeing that the main idea of this book is to break mental health down in layman's terms, I will explain the theories in a simplified way.

The biological theories mostly suggest two reasons for APD. One indicates that antisocial people have improper brain functions when it comes to excitement and thrill seeking. Therefore, individuals with APD seek more dangerous or risky situations (i.e., crime or drugs) to satisfy their craving for excitement, while a person without the disorder would partake in more prosocial activities for stimulation (i.e., video-gaming, art, or extreme sports). The other biological theory believes that APD is the result of abnormal levels of serotonin in certain regions in the brain, which are responsible for mood regulation and behavior.

And as you can imagine, a person's family environment is probably one of the first areas professionals look to when examining antisocial behavior. Environmental theories purport that most antisocial people have antisocial parents, and that antisocial people inherit their delinquent ways from their parents.

Some environmental theories say that children who are deprived of opportunities to form bonds, and trusting relationships, develop APD. This could be a child that was raised in the legal system or a child with cold, abusive parents. Some environmental philosophies suppose a lack of supervision in early childhood and inconsistent monitoring are significant factors in APD. Overall, most of the environmental models think that a child who grows up in a disturbed home may enter the adult world emotionally injured. And without having developed emotional bonds with his or her caregivers, he or she becomes self-absorbed and indifferent to others.

Frequency of Antisocial Personality Disorder/Conduct disorder

About 1-3% of the U.S. population has antisocial disorder[13]. Much higher percentages come from those within the legal system. Approximately 50-80% of the prison population is either officially diagnosed with APD or has shown symptoms of the disorder but has yet to have a doctor tell them they have APD[14]. And roughly 90% of those recognized as psychopaths are in the criminal justice system[15].

Conduct disorder —which is basically the childhood version of APD—is the most common mental health diagnosis in the juvenile justice system. Case studies on court-involved juveniles found that as high as 40% of juvenile offenders have conduct disorder[16].

One issue with the diagnosis of conduct disorder (and APD) within legal spheres is that people with these illnesses tend to get harsher sentences and other punitive actions that people with other mental illnesses don't. The fact that there is a bias against those with APD and conduct disorder fundamentally ensures that they will funnel in and out the legal system for years to come, as it's unlikely they'll get the help they need.

Risk Factors

APD has so many risk factors that it's impossible to list them all. So for efficiency's sake, I will only name the most common ones. To find other risk factors, a simple internet search should provide you with all the info you need.

- **An individual's temperament:** Temperament refers to an individual's emotions, activity, attention, and self-control capabilities that manifest in the period between infancy and the early school years. Children with difficult temperaments are at risk for APD and conduct disorder.

- **Family factors:** inconsistent supervision combined with harsh punishment, large family size (four or more), institutional living early in life, parental rejection, inconsistent parental figures (e.g., shifting from parents to grandparents), and the presence of an alcoholic father.

- **Aggression:** Aggression presenting during or before preschool years predict delinquency and antisocial acts.

- **Poor peer relationships:** People with poor peer relationships are subjected to rejection, and in turn, may seek out relationships with other socially deviant individuals, forming peer groups in which they may influence each other and intensify progression toward violent and criminal behavior.

- **A diagnosis of conduct disorder:** A diagnosis of conduct disorder is a risk factor for APD. Approximately 25-40% of kids with conduct disorder develop APD during adulthood[17].

- **Unemployment, coupled with pre-existing delinquent or antisocial tendencies:** Financial hardship can increase the likelihood that an adult will revert to their childhood problematic behavior (e.g., stealing, fraud) to sustain themselves.

Protective Factors

Personality factors: An individual's positive perception of their own self-control, cooperation, and social problem-solving skills can mitigate APD symptoms.

Active participation in school: Active involvement in school and extracurricular activities are key factors that protect an individual from falling into negative patterns of behavior, which can lead to antisocial behavior.

Socioeconomic status (SES): Above average, SES can serve as a buffer for protection against the development of antisocial tendencies. Though SES is not a determining factor in whether an individual develops antisocial tendencies, individuals of higher SES are statistically less likely to develop conduct disorder or APD.

Positive behavioral support or positive parenting: Parenting that is high in warmth, responsiveness, and compassion is essential in protecting against APD.

Inhibitory control: The ability to suppress and control inappropriate action. Inhibitory control is vital in the development of conscience, prosocial behavior, and the inhibition of antisocial behavior.

Case Example: Antisocial personality disorder

Background

Born to a single mother in West Baltimore, 20-year-old Johnathan, aka "J-baby," a high-school dropout, is the father of three children from three different women. Johnathan's mother had him when she was 16 years old. Having dealt with heroin and alcohol addiction most of her life, his mother was far from a "model" parent, and Johnathan's childhood was anything but pleasant for him and his three siblings.

Johnathan has a younger teenage brother and a 12-year-old sister. His older brother, "Roc," was murdered four years ago. Rumor has it his slaying was retaliation for a homicide he committed earlier that year.

Struggling with addiction, Johnathan's mother encouraged her children to commit crimes to support her habits. Johnathan and his older brother Roc got into a criminal lifestyle early. Johnathan and his siblings never met their father. Roc was the only father figure Johnathan had. By the time he was a teenager, Roc already had a reputation for being a "jackboy" (a robber) in the neighborhood. Occasionally, Roc took Johnathan on robberies to "show him the ropes" and teach him how to make money.

Impairment from Disorder

At twenty years old, Johnathan has never had a job or a legitimate way of making money. This is mainly because starting at age 13, the majority of his life has been spent in the legal system. But even if he could have had a job, he has never wanted nor attempted to get one. Juvenile detention, probation, and expulsions from school have never—even in the slightest bit—curbed his reckless behavior.

Countless counselors, teachers, and other authority figures have tried to get through to him, but their advice has gone in one ear and out the other. Johnathan is usually indifferent to anyone who tries to help him change his ways. The only people who have any influence on him are his friends, all of whom have extensive legal histories as well.

During his childhood, Johnathan was a bully and had been suspended from school dozens of times for fighting, drug abuse, and truancy. But eventually, he was expelled from school for getting caught with a weapon on school grounds.

As an adult, Johnathan's behaviors worsened. He smokes marijuana daily, drinks heavily, and abuses pain pills and cough syrup. When intoxicated, he bullies people and tends to be violent towards those who dare to stand up to him. Johnathan is a known drug dealer in West Baltimore. He has been involved in several robberies, assaults, and shootouts.

Johnathan shows no remorse for his actions. He brags on social media about his violent acts and calls himself "Bmore's top Shotta." Johnathan's criminal behavior is so excessive that even some of the people he commits crimes with think he's too reckless. Most people who know Johnathan would describe him as difficult, untrustworthy, and hotheaded.

Nearly all of his relationships are unstable. Johnathan doesn't have close relationships with any of his children, and he never sees the children by his own choice. Despite the efforts of his kids' mothers, he makes excuses to avoid the responsibility of being a parent.

Shortly after the birth of his third child, Johnathan was arrested and sentenced to ten years for robbery and kidnapping.

Mental Health Dx

Formal Diagnosis: Antisocial Personality Disorder

Justification for Dx

Disregard for society's laws: Johnathan is a career criminal. He is indifferent to those who have tried to steer him down the right path.

Violating the rights of others: Johnathan has a history of bullying, robbing, stealing, and violence.

Lack of stability in employment and home life: Johnathan has never held a legitimate job, primarily makes money through illegal activities. Also, he has an unstable relationship with his children (and their mothers) as he is an absent father.

Lack of remorse: Johnathan shows no sympathy about the harm he's caused others, often bragging about crimes on social media.

A childhood diagnosis of conduct disorder: Although never formally diagnosed, Johnathan exhibited many symptoms of conduct disorder during his childhood, such as bullying, stealing, frequent suspensions from school, and numerous run-ins with police.

Attention-Deficit/Hyperactivity Disorder (ADHD)

"Having a high IQ or being intelligent does not mean ADHD is not a disability."

–Y.T.

ADHD, in my opinion, is the most commonly misdiagnosed mental illness in the black community. Although many people legitimately have ADHD, it seems to be a one-size-fits-all, go-to diagnosis used by clinicians who either lack cultural awareness or are trying to meet insurance requirements for reimbursement. And due to the complexity and controversy of that issue, that's a conversation I won't delve into in this book. But for those who do actually have the disorder, seemingly ordinary tasks can seem like monumental feats. That said, people with this condition often have challenges in various areas of their lives.

What is ADHD?

ADHD is a complex brain disorder best described as a developmental impairment of self-management functions connected to complex brain operations. In layman's terms, ADHD impacts the executive functioning area in an individual's brain, which makes it difficult for them to assess, plan, and execute life. This means different things to different people. For some, ADHD only affects them in school settings. They might have trouble paying attention, while others may have a hard time sitting still for long periods and seem to have an endless supply of energy.

ADHD rarely looks the same for any two people. In fact, there are three different types of ADHD: Inattentive type, hyperactivity-impulsive type, and *combined* type. Those with inattentive ADHD have problems focusing. People with this type of ADHD often have poor grades in school and tend to make careless mistakes during daily activities. They are the type of people who seem like they just can't get it right. And I don't say this to speak ill of people with ADHD, but this is the reality of their condition.

Then there's hyperactivity-impulsive type ADHD, which is the ADHD that most people think of when we talk about ADHD. This is the hyperactive, bouncing off the wall, can't be quiet to save their life type of person. And the symptoms are usually much more pronounced in children than adults. Adults with ADHD tend to mature over time and learn to better manage their symptoms while children have yet to discover the coping skills required to deal with their condition, which is why you really only see children behaving in stereotypical hyperactive ADHD ways.

Kids with ADHD often are seen as "bad kids" because adults, such as teachers and parents, usually don't realize that the child's behavior is due to a mental health issue. Adults tend to believe the children's actions are due to bad parenting or the kid's natural inclination towards attention-seeking behavior. Yes, it is true that ADHD kids, just as any other kid, can simply be a "bad kid" but it's important to rule out ADHD as the cause of the "bad" behavior first, before taking the same disciplinary measures as you would with an actual "bad kid."

Lack of Focus

Many who have inattentive type ADHD are forgetful, have short attention spans, and make careless mistakes. Inattentive ADHD makes the simplest tasks seem demanding. Clients of mine say it's very discouraging to struggle with things that most people can do with ease. ADHD children often come to therapy because their parents have grown so frustrated with their child's failure to follow through with basic instructions that they need professional assistance. ADHD is not always as apparent as you'd think. Laziness, lack of ambition, and/or stubbornness are usually thought of as the problem way before people even suspect ADHD. Furthermore, quiet and well-mannered children often never get diagnosed with the condition or receive an extremely delayed diagnosis because they don't exhibit the stereotypical ADHD personality.

Adults with ADHD struggle with inattentiveness too. It usually plays out in work settings. Inattentiveness at work doesn't sound like it is a big deal. We all lack focus at times, right? Yes, but chances are the boss doesn't know or care if their employee has ADHD—they want results. And often, ADHD makes performing work obligations seem impossible.

The effects of ADHD can spill over into other areas of life. People have lost relationships, jobs, and experienced extreme humiliation—all in the name of ADHD. Some people even end up developing other mental illnesses like depression or anxiety due to internalizing negative thoughts about themselves based on their disability. And what a lot of people don't know is ADHD is, indeed, a disability. We must change the paradigm in which we see this condition.

Think about it this way, if your child had asthma or diabetes, or some other physical ailment, would you, for one second, hesitate to advocate for him or her? Just as a diabetic needs insulin, and an asthmatic child needs an inhaler, a child with ADHD needs his learning environment regulated. One of the best ways to reduce ADHD symptoms is to organize a schedule that gets the individual into a routine so that daily tasks are second nature, as it's easy for folks with ADHD to get off track.

Honestly, people with ADHD are no less intelligent than anyone else, but the way their brain operates causes them to have a much shorter attention span, which is the reason why they tend to struggle with simple tasks that involve attention to detail or prolonged focus.

The Problem Child

Kids with ADHD get a bad rap. Teachers, parents, and a myriad of other authority figures cringe at the thought of dealing with children with ADHD. And the problem with that sort of thinking is that very few adults actually understand what ADHD is, and consequently are ill equipped to manage its symptoms. Almost all of my school-based referrals for therapy are based on ADHD symptoms (I suspect the same would be true for most therapists). Possibly the most predominant school-related issue regarding the behavior of students with ADHD is trying to contain the hyperactive student. Simply telling them to stop being disruptive is not going to work. Believe it or not, they can't help but keep getting out of their seat or blurting things out in class several times per day.

People with Hyperactive ADHD (especially children) cannot stay still for long periods. They are antsy and restless. They may talk non-stop, even after you tell them to be quiet; they just cannot stop. And to most people it may seem like defiance (which in some cases it is), but most people with ADHD mean well, they just can't control their energy level. Medication is an excellent way to manage hyperactivity. But one must not be reliant on medicine because medicine alone won't solve the problem. Learning coping skills to mitigate ADHD's symptoms, in conjunction with medication is the best way to help a child with ADHD.

What are the Symptoms of ADHD?

The common symptoms of ADHD are:

Mental

- **Inattention:** lack of focus or short attention span.
- **Poor listening skills**: not seeming to listen when spoken to directly.
- **Has problems organizing tasks and activities**: such as what to do in sequence, keeping materials and belongings in order, having messy work and poor time-management, and failing to meet deadlines.

Behavioral

- **Irresponsibleness**: Regularly losing things necessary for tasks or activities, such as school supplies, pencils, books, tools, wallets, keys, paperwork, eyeglasses, and cell phones.
- **Avoids or dislikes tasks that require continual mental effort**: such as schoolwork or homework. Teens and adults may dislike and avoid preparing reports, completing forms, or reviewing lengthy papers.
- **Carelessness:** overlooks or misses details, makes careless mistakes in schoolwork, at work, or during other activities. Or is forgetful in daily activities such as chores, errands, returning calls, and keeping appointments.
- **Fidgets and squirms**: cannot sit still for extended periods.
- **Talkativeness:** talks non-stop.
- **Disorderliness:** runs, dashes, or climbs in inappropriate situations, or feels restless and unable to play or engage in hobbies quietly.
- **Highly active:** constantly in motion or "on the go," or acts as if "driven by a motor."
- **Interrupt or intrude on others**: can't wait for his or her turn in conversations, games, or activities.

Physical

- There are not many physical symptoms of ADHD. For the most part, the symptoms are considered behavioral (i.e., fidgeting, restlessness, etc.).

What Causes ADHD?

There is not a single cause for ADHD. However, both environmental and biological circumstances do seem to lead to the disorder. From scientific studies, it has been found that the brains of youth with ADHD look and function somewhat differently than the brains of an ordinary developing child[18]. Deficits in the brains of people with ADHD cause an inability to manage their attention and impulsivity effectively.

Environmental factors, such as smoking or drug abuse during pregnancy, can lead to ADHD. Improper prenatal care is a known factor leading to the development of this condition. Many parents of ADHD children were irresponsible during their pregnancy. I'm not saying it is always the mother's behavior that leads to the disorder, but prenatal care is definitely worth mentioning when talking about causes for this disorder.

Other circumstances within the home can worsen ADHD for those who already have the condition. Harsh and inconsistent parenting can aggravate ADHD symptoms. An example of this would be a parent who scolds and reprimands a child for not cleaning their room sometimes and says nothing other times. The best way to manage ADHD is through methods that implement consistency, structure, and above all—empathy.

Frequency of ADHD

About 1 in 20 children have ADHD[19]. And boys are three times more likely to develop ADHD than girls. The symptoms are more pronounced with boys because boys usually are more active than girls, which is a possible explanation for the increased prevalence in boys. Girls with ADHD may be more likely to be overlooked because their symptoms are less obvious, even though they may have as much difficulty as boys with academic and social skills.

Adolescents with the disorder have nearly identical numbers regarding prevalence. Teen males are three times as likely to have ADHD, just like younger kids with ADHD. The only distinction between childhood ADHD and teen ADHD is that teens of both genders display more symptoms than children, which means that their ADHD is more severe.

Five percent of adult males and three percent of adult females have ADHD. The overall prevalence amongst all adults in the U.S. is about eight percent. These numbers don't even consider that many people don't know they have ADHD. Therefore, they haven't been formally diagnosed, which makes the total percentage of ADHD seem significantly smaller than it actually is.

Risk Factors

Genes: ADHD is known to be inherited in families. It is often passed down from generation to generation.

Inadequate prenatal care: smoking, alcohol use, drug use, or other reckless behavior during pregnancy.

Exposure to environmental toxins: such as high levels of lead, at a young age, or during pregnancy.

Developmental issues: i.e., low birth weight or learning disabilities.

Protective Factors

Social acceptance: Even though it sounds relatively shallow, acceptance from peers and meaningful friendships helps protect against ADHD.

Positive parenting: Parents that are consistent, emotionally stable, and empathetic help prevent ADHD. Also, for youth with ADHD or similar symptoms, positive parenting may be an essential source of social support and social modeling, leading to reduced problems in interactions with peers and teachers.

Positive self-perception: The way individuals view themselves has an impact on their reaction to stress. People with a positive self-concept are hopeful about their future, believe in their ability to influence their circumstances, and are confident they can overcome obstacles.

Case Example: Attention-Deficit/ Hyperactivity Disorder

Background

Marshay has always had trouble getting her son, Devontae, to behave. From the time he was a toddler up to present day, 16-year-old Devontae has had problems following directions. According to Marshay, Devontae is a good kid; he just can't focus long enough to get things done. Marshay says that she has the same problem, and it was even worse when she was Devontae's age. Devontae's dad, Rick, believes that he is just lazy and doesn't want to do anything other than play videogames and watch TV all day. Rick thinks that Devontae can follow directions on the videogames so he should be able to follow them at home and school.

Impairment from Disorder

In school, Devontae's problems seem to intensify. Not only does he not pay attention, but he is also disruptive and seems to have an endless supply of energy. Devontae spends considerable time each day in the main office at school. His teacher sends him there just to get a break from his antics.

For most of the other students, staying seated or remaining quiet during learning time is a relatively simple task, but for Devontae, it's nearly impossible. Devontae's teachers report that he is very active and doesn't follow directions; they have to tell him to be quiet or escort him to his seat several times each day. During lessons, Devontae often blurts out answers without raising his hand, even after his teacher asks him not to. Teachers often seclude him from the rest of the class to prevent him from interrupting instruction. When isolated, he will squirm in his seat and fidget with his pencil and papers to keep himself busy.

When Devontae isn't disrupting the class, he is usually daydreaming. His teachers say he spends a considerable amount of the day in "la-la land" because it seems like he is in a trance, the way he drifts off. Sometimes, a teacher might call his name three or four times before he responds.

Although his behavior is undoubtedly troublesome for school staff and other students, Devontae's mother insists that his disruptiveness isn't malicious. She believes that he simply can't help himself.

At home, Devontae is very messy. His parents describe his room as a "disaster." For Devontae, doing chores is a daily struggle; either he doesn't do them at all, or he needs constant supervision to ensure the job is done right. His father believes that he is lazy and doesn't have the discipline to uphold household responsibilities. Whereas his mother, recognizing the pattern from her own childhood behaviors, believes there may be a more serious cause for his behavior.

Mental Health Dx

Formal Diagnosis: Attention-Deficit/Hyperactivity Disorder, combined presentation, mild.

Justification for Dx

Time period of symptoms: since early childhood.

Inattentiveness: trance-like daydreaming, can't focus in school or at home.

Easily distracted: can't stay on task without supervision.

Talks excessively: blurts out things in class. Even though he means no harm, Devontae can't be quiet during times when he is expected to.

Hyperactivity: fidgets and squirms when seated for long periods, extremely energetic.

Struggles with activities that require sustained attention: schoolwork, chores, etc.

Poor organizational skills: keeping room clean can be a challenge.

Posttraumatic Stress Disorder (PTSD)

"PTSD: It's not the person refusing to let go of the past, but the past refusing to let go of the person."

—Unknown

PTSD is one of the few disorders that can be connected to an exact situation; it's different from other mental illnesses because it's explicitly based on trauma. And not just any trauma, but a life-threatening experience. The other disorders I have addressed are usually based on less-severe situations that don't necessarily classify as "trauma" (well, at least not when it comes to being diagnosed with PTSD).

What is PTSD?

PTSD is a complex mental illness caused by trauma. The trauma can be direct or indirect, meaning the ordeal can be something that has happened to a person or something a person has witnessed. Most people who have PTSD have experienced trauma directly, but there are lots of people who develop PTSD from seeing something happen to someone else. Sometimes, just hearing about a devastating event can be enough to cause PTSD.

When people think of trauma, they usually think about witnessing a murder, being raped, or surviving a car accident. And each of those events undoubtedly qualifies as trauma. But it doesn't necessarily have to be something done at the hands of another person. Sometimes events like natural disasters (i.e., a hurricane or tornado) lead to PTSD symptoms. PTSD can also come from a severe illness like cancer, or an injury, for instance, a broken bone; direct or indirect experiences of these predicaments can also bring about PTSD symptoms.

PTSD affects how you feel in several ways. It can impact your personal relationships, ability to work, even your sleeping and eating patterns. PTSD's most distinctive features involve re-experiencing a traumatic situation (e.g., flashbacks, nightmares, intrusive thoughts, etc.), avoidance of triggering situations, or hyperarousal (feeling on edge or jumpy).

It's tough for people with PTSD to live their lives without being triggered somehow. Sometimes women who were victims of sexual assault have difficulty dating and enjoying sex with their lovers because they are triggered by disturbing events from their past. Or people who have witnessed violent crime may be triggered by TV shows that remind them of the incident. Some people go to great lengths to avoid anything that's potentially triggering. Imagine living your life in fear of being triggered, trying to duck and dodge potential reminders of traumatic circumstances. That's no way to live. In theory, avoiding triggers sounds like a practical solution to solve the problem of PTSD. But in reality, all it does is make the fear more formidable.

PTSD extends Beyond the Battlefield

Because not many people outside of the mental health field really understand PTSD, people tend to think PTSD *only* happens to war vets and police officers. But the vast majority of cases of PTSD do not involve servicemen and women. The sufferers are usually average, everyday folk, who live ordinary lives. Believe it or not, rape is a common cause of the disorder. To have someone force you into sex—the most intimate action two people can participate in—can definitely leave emotional wounds that can't be easily healed.

Another frequent, but at the same time, overlooked, source of PTSD is community violence. I must touch on this source of PTSD for people who live in high-crime neighborhoods where murders, brutal fistfights, shootouts, amongst many other disturbing things happen on the regular. Violence in high-crime communities is so ordinary that a lot of people are desensitized to it because they never get to process it adequately. They're numb to it, and they don't fully grasp the cumulative emotional toll that these events take on them over time. And the problem with that is, just because they don't process their trauma doesn't mean that the effects don't remain. In other words, there are a lot of black folks who are carrying the burden of PTSD and don't know it.

Survivor's Remorse

People with PTSD often feel guilty about surviving a dangerous situation that others did not, or feel guilty about what they had to do to survive. David, one of the first clients I saw in my clinical internship during grad school, talked about losing his younger brother due to an accident at a swimming pool when he was a kid. David said he always felt like he should have been the one who drowned, and that his younger brother didn't deserve to die. Up until he saw me for treatment, David spent most of his life beating himself up, believing that his lack of professional accomplishments and personal achievements somehow meant his brother died in vain.

That's such a toxic way of thinking. But those were the thoughts that ran through David's mind on a daily basis.

No amount of success will bring back someone from the dead. Nor is any amount of failure justification for you to take the place of the deceased. You must accept what is and strive to move forward with your life. The sooner you commit to acceptance, the sooner you can recover emotionally.

PTSD Can Hijack Your Mind

Following a traumatic episode, it's hard to get your mind to go back to normal. It seems as if it has been hijacked. Your brain no longer does what you want it to do—which is to forget the trauma. After trauma, adrenalin and other neurochemicals rush to the brain and print an image of the horrific situation there. The traumatic memory repeatedly loops in the emotional side of the brain, disconnecting from the part of the brain that does reasoning and cognitive processing. The reasonable portion of the brain is unable to help the emotionally loaded part of the brain move past from the trauma. As a result, the brain can be easily triggered by normal, non-threatening things. For example, fireworks are no longer fireworks, now it's a possible explosion. A girl traumatized by rape no longer views her boyfriend as her lover. He now reminds her of the man who did the rape. When these types of incidents happen, the brain loses its ability to discriminate between danger and what is normal.

What Are the Symptoms of PTSD?

The most common symptoms of PTSD are:

Mental

- **Sleep disturbances:** nightmares and graphic dreams based on a disturbing incident.
- **Freighting thoughts:** being scared by the very idea of a past traumatic situation or fearing it happening again.
- **Flashbacks:** vivid images of the trauma. Flashbacks can seem very real, and some people describe them as a picture or a movie that they can see clearly in their minds.
- **Easily triggered:** reminded of trauma by words, objects, or situations that may or may not be related to the initial incident.

- **Irritability:** angry outbursts or moodiness with little provocation.
- **Guilt:** believing the incident was your fault, even if it wasn't.

Behavioral

- **Avoidance:** Staying away from places, events, or objects that are reminders of the experience, or avoiding thoughts or feelings that may be reminiscent of the event.
- **Easily startled:** jumpy or on edge for no apparent reason.
- **Hypervigilance:** excessive caution to protect against danger, or unnecessarily worrying about the safety of others.
- **Sleep disturbances:** difficulty sleeping or sleeping more than usual.
- **Bedwetting (children):** wetting the bed after being potty-trained.
- **Acting out event (children):** may enact traumatic situations during playtime.
- **Self-destructive behavior:** drinking excessively, taking drugs, suicidal or self-injurious behaviors, or constant involvement with the law.

Physical

- **Increased heart rate:** heart pounding when thinking about the traumatic event.
- **Sweating:** sweating when thinking about the event or situations that may trigger the event.
- **Feeling sick:** wanting to throw up or feeling nauseous.

What causes PTSD?

It is not known, *specifically*, what causes the brain to act the way it does when it's traumatized, but the events that lead to PTSD are relatively simple. Preexisting psychological and biological components, as well as the existence of a traumatic event, form the recipe that causes PTSD. Unlike a phobia (fear of mice, heights, clowns, etc.), which is based on learned knowledge, PTSD is based on a single chain of events. When someone discovers they can fall off a building and die, they may develop a fear of heights. Or a creepy experience with a clown as a child may eventually lead to a clown phobia. Neither of those phobias is based on a life-threating situation, which is a key feature of PTSD. With PTSD, the fear is more primal (based on instincts) rather than due to something learned. PTSD is more of a complication of a disturbing event that happens spontaneously, while phobias are a deeply rooted fear that is learned, and festers over time.

Frequency of PTSD

PTSD is a relatively common mental illness, as 6.8% of the United States population will have PTSD at some point in their lives[20]. While that doesn't sound like a lot, that means, basically, 7 out of every 100 people. So chances are you know at least 7 people with PTSD. That's nothing to take lightly. Given the severity of PTSD, 7% is way too high. And women are twice as likely as men to have the disorder because women are generally more vulnerable to trauma than men.

PTSD is not uncommon for children either. Individuals under the age of 18 experience PTSD at a rate of 4%. The National Center of Mental Health says that around 7% of girls and 2% of boys will develop PTSD at some point in their lives.

Black people have low rates when it comes to anxiety disorders compared to other races. But PTSD is the one anxiety disorder that is exceptionally prevalent with blacks[21]. This elevated rate is likely due to our increased exposure to high trauma environments. Growing up in a dangerous community means that it's more likely that you will experience some kind of trauma, which can cause PTSD.

Risk Factors

It is important to remember that not everyone who lives through a life-threating event develops PTSD; actually, most people don't have any symptoms at all. Many factors play a part in whether someone will develop PTSD, such as:

Witnessing or being a victim to a life-threating event: such as a shooting, stabbing, or beating. Also, seeing a dead body, a rape, and car accidents are common sources of PTSD.

Severe Illness or injuries: Cancer, strokes, or a heart attack can put someone at risk for PTSD. Also, severe injuries like a broken neck or a torn ligament can increase the risk for the disorder.

Natural Disasters: Experience of a hurricane, tornado, and earthquake increases the likelihood of PTSD.

Stress after trauma: dealing with extra stress after the event, such as loss of a loved one, pain and injury, or loss of a job or home.

Substance Abuse: A history of addiction to drugs and alcohol increases the risk of PTSD.

Protective Factors

Supportive influences: seeking support from friends, family, or support groups following the trauma.

Positive coping skills: learning strategies to help reduce anxious feelings surrounding the traumatic event.

Mental health treatment: Seeking treatment from qualified mental health professionals can help protect against PTSD.

Case Example: Posttraumatic Stress Disorder

Background

Ebony, age 21, a single mother of two from Texas, to her knowledge, has never had any real issues. Her mother and father are married and have a loving relationship. Her childhood, for the most part, was relatively uneventful. If you were to ask Ebony, outside of raising two children on her own, she has never had anything terrible happen to her—until the unthinkable happened.

Impairment from Disorder

Ebony has always been a socially active person, regularly hanging out and going to parties with her friends. At every event, she is the life of the party. All the girls want to hang with her, and all the guys want a chance to get to know her. One guy wanted her so badly that he wouldn't take no for an answer.

After a night of partying, a man approached Ebony as she was fumbling with her keys, trying to get into her apartment.

"Aye, can I talk to you for a minute, Ma?" the man asked.

Ebony responded with her usual, polite way of rejecting men that approach her, saying in a warm, humble tone, "Sorry, I have a boyfriend."

The man replied, "So that means you can't have friends?" as he approached her, intruding into her personal space.

Ebony, still fumbling with the keys, replied to the man softly, "No, goodnight," hoping he would get the hint.

As Ebony finally got the door open, the man simultaneously forced himself into her apartment and immediately tried to take her clothes off. Ebony attempted to fight the intruder off, but he overpowered her. She screamed, but the man told her, "If you don't be quiet, I'm going to blow your motherf**king head off!" as he roughly pressed a chrome revolver under her chin. At that point, Ebony stopped struggling, as she knew resistance was futile, and pleaded with the intruder not to kill her. The man pulled Ebony's pants down and began to have sex with her. The entire event lasted about 15 minutes, but it felt like a lifetime to Ebony.

After the event, Ebony was not the same. She would always seem mentally "checked out," and if not that, she would be on edge, as if preparing herself for something terrible to happen. It is challenging for Ebony to go into her apartment without thinking about the attack, sometimes having flashbacks so detailed that she can smell the liquor on her attacker's breath, just as she did the day it happened.

The flashbacks are so realistic they're unbearable because they make her feel like she is reliving the situation. Ebony has intrusive thoughts about that night that seem impossible to shake. She usually avoids situations and people that may be potential triggers. She evades triggers so much that she avoids going home sometimes because fumbling her keys to get into her apartment may lead to an upsetting flashback, as it has many times in the past.

Mental Health Dx

Formal Diagnosis: Posttraumatic Stress Disorder

Justification for Dx

Near-death experience: Ebony encountered a life-threating situation, a rape, in which the attacker threated to kill her.

Emotional triggering: Ebony is frequently reminded of the trauma (e.g., when entering her apartment).

Hypervigilance: Ebony is "on edge" or guarded, as if she expects something terrible to happen.

Dissociative reactions (flashbacks): Ebony has intrusive thoughts or feels like the event is reoccurring.

Avoidance: Ebony avoids situations that may potentially remind her of the attack.

Schizophrenia

"There are a number of things that family and friends can do to help a person with schizophrenia. One of the simplest and most effective is to create a positive environment around the person."

—Milt Greek

Schizophrenia is probably the most stereotyped mental illness. When most people think about mental illness, schizophrenia is usually what they have in mind. Many people with this condition are viewed as "crazy" or dangerous (which is rarely the case) because its symptoms are odd and usually very noticeable.

What is Schizophrenia?

Schizophrenia is a brain disorder that alters a person's perception of reality. Many people with schizophrenia have a hard time separating real life and fantasy, managing emotions, and making decisions. Individuals with this condition have a vastly unusual thinking style and often have little motivation to do things that most people do daily, like work, or maintain good hygiene.

Schizophrenia distorts all of the body's senses. It isn't uncommon for someone with this illness to hear voices in their head that are not their own; or to see nonexistent objects or people. Some schizophrenics have reported unbelievably bizarre hallucinations like seeing dead relatives or gigantic spiders.

Seeing and hearing aren't the only ways schizophrenics hallucinate. Schizophrenia has been known to cause people to *smell* things that aren't present, like flowers or hazardous materials such as chemicals. This type of hallucination is potentially dangerous as it may lead to refusing to eat out of fear of being poisoned. Hallucinations also appear as feelings of movement or bodily sensations that aren't actually present, like hands touching your body or feeling bugs crawling on your skin when they really aren't.

Just because you may have hallucinated before doesn't necessarily mean you have schizophrenia, though. People with mood disorders, schizoaffective disorders, and other physical and mental health conditions may also hallucinate. Hallucinations can also happen when under the influence of drugs or alcohol.

Menace to Society

Schizophrenic people tend to be *labeled* as "crazy", or even worse—dangerous. I have seen countless people with this disorder cycle in and out of jail for petty "crimes" like disorderly conduct or loitering. Most of the time, people call the police on schizophrenics because their odd behavior makes them uncomfortable. They don't understand that schizophrenics are not dangerous. They just behave and process information differently, see and hear things that aren't really there, and sometimes dress oddly (such as wearing a winter coat in the summer).

Typically, police encounters involving people with mental illness don't go well. Police, just like most civilians, don't really have much mental health awareness, which is usually the reason why police misunderstand psychological crises and consider the behavior to be noncompliance or criminal behavior.

Compromised Living Skills

Schizophrenia can affect the way someone thinks. So, that means it can influence how they take care of themselves. Because of the intensity of Schizophrenia, many people are abandoned by their families and other support systems. This is why you see a lot of homeless people with this illness. In many cases, the stigmatization of schizophrenia is so strong that even loved ones can't see past the symptoms, and recognize this as an illness that requires compassion and support to survive.

Battling Schizophrenia alone is nearly impossible. If you know someone with schizophrenia, help them find necessary support systems (i.e., mental health clinics, psych nurses, group homes, etc.). Avoiding or shaming them will only make their symptoms worse. The more help a person receives, the fewer complications they will have with this disorder. Although schizophrenia can never be cured, with support, the symptoms can be managed, and the person can go on to live a happy and productive life.

Out of Touch with Reality

Schizophrenic hallucinations can alter a person's sense of reality. They often have illusionary experiences that are well beyond a vivid imagination. The mind of a schizophrenic is vastly distorted.

People with schizophrenia describe hallucinations of hearing strange noises like clicks or other non-word sounds. But occasionally, the noises are in the form of words. And the words range from reassuring or kind words to aggravating, unpleasant, or derogatory terms. Sometimes, the words themselves are not necessarily directed at the person, but the words concern them in an unclear way.

Schizophrenics also have *delusional thoughts*. Delusions differ from hallucinations in that hallucinations are *sensed* (seen, heard, smelled, etc.) but are not real. Whereas delusions are strongly held *beliefs* that are completely false. It's typical for schizophrenic people to have persecutory thoughts, like thinking someone is out to get them; grandiose ideas, such as believing they have superpowers or relationships with celebrities they've never met. People with this condition have weird beliefs despite there being substantial evidence that there's no truth to their ideas. For instance, someone believing he is married to Beyoncé. Either this is a clear example of a delusion; the person in question is Jay-Z… or Beyoncé's got some explaining to do!

What are the Symptoms of Schizophrenia?

Schizophrenia symptoms fall into three categories: positive, negative, and cognitive. The meaning of positive and negative symptoms is not in the literal sense when it comes to schizophrenia. Positive symptoms are any behaviors that are generally not seen in healthy individuals. Negative symptoms are the loss of particular abilities, such as loss of skills or behaviors that are present in healthy individuals. And cognitive symptoms are problems with an individual's overall thought process.

The most common symptoms of Schizophrenia are:

Positive

- **Hallucinations:** sensing things that aren't actually present (i.e., seeing or hearing things that aren't really there).
- **Delusions:** having abnormal beliefs that aren't simple misunderstandings, but instead, are a complete distortion of reality.
- **Movement Disorders:** experiencing unusual or seemingly useless movements. Some schizophrenics have tics (jumpy movements). Some people may move their mouths as if they are chewing, or appear agitated or distressed.

Negative

- **Lack of Facial Expressions and Emotion:** People with negative schizophrenic symptoms show limited emotional expressions. They might have a blank facial expression or an oddly plain tone of voice.

- **Reduced Speaking:** People with negative schizophrenic symptoms often won't speak, even when spoken to directly, as if they are ignoring a speaker.
- **Lack of Motivation:** People with negative schizophrenic symptoms have difficulty beginning and continuing activities.

Cognitive

- **Poor Executive Functioning:** the ability to understand information and use it to make decisions.
- **Concentration Issues:** trouble focusing or paying attention
- **Memory Issues:** may easily forget things, even within a short period.

What Causes Schizophrenia?

There is no absolute cause of schizophrenia. It has been known for a long time that schizophrenia runs in families. Most of the research on this disorder supports the idea that schizophrenia is caused by genetics. However, many schizophrenics don't have a family member with the disorder. And, equally, lots of people with one or more family members with schizophrenia do not develop it themselves.

It's also a possibility that defects in brain development are the reason for the condition. Some experts think that issues during brain development, while a child is still in the womb, can also cause schizophrenia.

Frequency of Schizophrenia

You'd think, from all of the homeless schizophrenic people you've seen on the streets throughout your life, that schizophrenia is a terribly common disorder. But schizophrenia is not all that common. Worldwide, there is only a one percent rate for schizophrenia. And in the United States, the rate is about the same. Approximately 1.5 million people will be diagnosed with schizophrenia this year around the world.

In the United States, this means about 100,000 people will be diagnosed, which translates to 7.2 people per 1,000 or about 21,000 people within a city of 3 million who will likely to suffer from schizophrenia[22].

Although schizophrenia affects people at different times throughout their lifespan, it's rare for someone to develop it during childhood or old age. Most instances of schizophrenia happen during the late teens or early adulthood, but it's possible to develop it at any age. The best thing to do if you suspect a person might be schizophrenic is to get a second opinion from an expert.

Risk Factors

Researchers believe a combination of a person's genes and their environment is the primary source of risk factors for schizophrenia. Below are a few risk factors associated with schizophrenia:

Exposure to viruses and toxins: exposure to viruses such as herpes and toxins like lead.

Malnutrition before birth: mothers who don't engage in proper prenatal care (i.e., smoking, eating unhealthy foods, or starvation).

Family environment: Genetics play a huge role in the development of this condition. Those who have family with schizophrenia are at an increased risk of developing it themselves.

Developmental issues: hormonal imbalances, deformities in brain development during pregnancy or early childhood, as well as complications during birth or pregnancy.

Protective Factors

Proper care during pregnancy: Focusing on lowering the incidence of complications during pregnancy can serve as a protective factor.

Abstinence from street drugs and alcohol: Significant drug and alcohol abuse have been known to cause brain damage and increase risk.

Case Example: Schizophrenia

Background

Dion, age 27, is described by his friends and family as an odd man. Mostly because of his unusual interests and limited social skills. In high school, Dion was an average student, but was artistically talented, as he would sometimes draw realistic portraits of his friends. Dion didn't have many close friends but did date occasionally. His mother didn't support him having friends.

Dion and his mother had a rocky relationship. She was cold and nasty toward him and his younger brother. According to Dion, she would call them names like "stupid" or "ugly" and would humiliate them if they made even the most minor mistakes. It's rumored that her father (Dion's grandfather) would beat her and her siblings bloody, almost daily, up until the day he died. His mother did not talk much about her father, but according to Dion, her father had "mental issues."

Impairment from Disorder

After high school, Dion's hygiene started to slip. He would go days, if not weeks, without bathing or brushing his teeth; his family usually had to make him do these things because he would not do them on his own.

Around age 18, Dion started to notice that he was hearing voices in his head that were not his own. At first, he could barely understand what they were saying, but over time, the voices became louder and clearer. The voices often said mean, offensive things to him. Allegedly, the voices once told him he should kill himself. Sometimes, Dion was able to handle the voices in his head by ignoring them, but there were times when they stressed him to the point where he would argue with them aloud. Occasionally, he would be seen walking through his neighborhood, talking to himself—sometimes, yelling and cussing.

As he got older, his symptoms got worse. Not only did he hear voices, but he also began to believe people were "out to get him."

Dion had a part-time job at an electronics store. However, his employment was short-lived because he told all of the customers that the company had planted a bug in his brain to monitor his thoughts. Shortly after, Dion was admitted into a psychiatric hospital.

Mental Health Dx

Formal Diagnosis: Schizophrenia

Justification for Dx

Strange behaviors: inability to thrive socially.

Poor Hygiene: Dion's hygiene began to slip around his 18th birthday. Dion doesn't bathe or brush his teeth unless forced by family.

Audio Hallucinations: Dion was hearing voices in his head that were not his own. At times, the voices were argumentative and threating, telling him to harm himself.

Delusions: Dion was convinced that his employer was spying on him by monitoring his thoughts.

Autism Spectrum Disorder (ASD or Autism)

"Autism is part of my child. It's not everything he is. My child is so much more than a diagnosis."

–S.L. Coelho

Like schizophrenia, Autism spectrum disorder (ASD) or "autism" is not a disorder that is relatively common but still is one of the most stigmatized and stereotyped mental illnesses. The general stereotypes for it are; either the person is incredibly low functioning (someone who can't take care of himself) or the total opposite —a peculiar individual with savant-like intelligence. Some people could fit either of those descriptions, but the truth is most people fall somewhere in the middle of the spectrum.

What is Autism?

Autism is a developmental illness that impairs the way someone expresses and recognizes emotion. It can also affect an individual's social skills. Autistic people often have odd ways of communicating and tend to exhibit strange behaviors. Most autistic people have unique personality types. Some may be loud and outgoing, while others can be quiet and reserved. But nearly all autistic people either have *social communication issues* and/or *repetitive behaviors.*

Unusual Behavioral Patterns

Repetitive behaviors are a hallmark trait of ASD. For instance, you may see an autistic man flapping his hands while he is talking, rocking back and forth, or walking on tiptoes in an uncoordinated way. Sometimes, autistic people repeat words multiple times in a sentence. Or you might hear them repeat the last word each time someone stops speaking. For example, if I say, "I had a good time today at church," they will randomly say "church." This is called *echolalia*. It isn't considered echolalia if someone repeats something in the correct context of a conversation. Echolalia occurs when a word is unnaturally or meaninglessly repeated after being heard. This is a fairly easy behavior to notice, but ask a counselor if you think this may be an issue for you or a loved one.

Missing Social Cues

At times, having a conversation with an autistic person can be challenging. Individuals with this condition have difficulty recognizing non-verbal expressions. To the average person, when someone rolls their eyes, it's considered sign language for *you're getting on my last damn nerve!* Or if someone asks a question that you don't know the answer to, and you shrug your shoulders, most people will intuitively understand what that non-verbal gesture means. But those with autism tend to miss these obvious social cues completely.

Empathy is another noteworthy social deficiency amongst the ASD population. That is not to say that they are coldhearted or cruel; their minds just work differently. Autistic people tend to struggle with *theory of mind.* Basically, what this means is that they don't have a strong ability to read people. If you've ever spent time with someone who's autistic, you might have noticed that they don't really hold their tongue. They pretty much say whatever's on their mind. I'm not saying that autistic people are more genuine than the average person; they can be rude or shallow just like anyone else. What I'm saying is that autistic people (in most cases) can't effectively predict what someone may be thinking or feeling based on personal experience or common knowledge.

Most people would probably understand that telling someone that they need to lose weight is rude and would probably hurt a person's feelings. Autistic people have a mental blind spot when it comes to social etiquette, and they usually say or do socially unacceptable things.

Childhood Autism

Most of the time, signs of autism become apparent in the early years of childhood. Just as with autistic adults, children with autism have some of the same problems with communication and social skills. A mental health professional can tell if a child is autistic because they may begin to show signs as early as 8-10 months old.

Not responding to his or her name by the time they've reached one-year-old is an indicator of the disorder. Most kids learn their name before their first birthday. Although they may not be able to say their name, they should respond when someone is talking to them.

Showing a preference to be alone is also a sign of childhood autism. No, it doesn't mean that a child is autistic because they are shy or introverted. But if the child's isolation seems more like they're ignoring everyone rather than expressing a preference for seclusion, it may be due to autism.

Almost half of autistic children don't talk at all. And about a quarter of the children learn language skills as a baby but lose them later. Some kids with ASD don't learn to talk until much later than what's considered normal for kids their age.

What are the Symptoms of Autism Spectrum Disorder?

ASD symptoms are divided into two categories: Social/communication problems and repetitive behavior.

The most common symptoms of ASD are:

Social/communication

- **Poor social skills:** problems with social interactions, such as sharing emotions at unusual times, may not recognize discomfort or frustration in others. Also, can be overly blunt or end conversations abruptly.

- **Odd facial expression:** may make facial expressions that don't go with what is being said (such as an angry face when not upset or smiling when agitated).
- **Problems with relationships:** Though it may not be true for all, many autistic people have trouble developing and maintaining friendships and romantic relationships.

Repetitive behavior

- **Repetitive movements, motions, or speech patterns:** repeating words in conversations for no apparent reason; flapping hands, blinking excessively, or rocking back and forth.
- **Rigid thinking or behaviors:** very stubborn about changing up routines or behaviors (i.e., always has to put clothes on in the same order, which may not necessarily be the most productive way of doing it).
- **Sensitivity towards sensory surroundings:** may have an increased or decreased sensitivity towards lights, certain sounds, smells, or even may like to touch and feel items in an unusual way.
- **Unusual interests:** Being fixated on objects or odd hobbies such as playing with inanimate objects as if they are toys.

What Causes Autism Spectrum Disorder?

There is no specific cause for autism. Given the complicated nature of this condition, symptoms and severity differ from person to person; both genetics and environment likely play a significant role in its development.

On the genetic side of things, ASD can be associated with a genetic disorder like *Rett syndrome* or *fragile X* syndrome. For other children, genetic mutations (defects) can affect brain development or cause brain cells not to work properly. Some brain cell dysfunction is inherited while other deficiencies seem to happen spontaneously.

When it comes to environmental causes, factors such as viral infections, pollution, and complications during pregnancies can lead to autism.

Frequency of Autism Spectrum Disorder

Although it is not as common of an illness as depression or PTSD, autism is still a relatively common mental disorder. I could be wrong, but I think most of us went to school with or knew autistic people in our neighborhood. In fact, Centers for Disease Control and Prevention (CDC) estimates 1 out of 59 children were diagnosed with autism in 2019. CDC also reported that ASD is four times more likely to occur with boys than it is with girls. The rate for boys is 1 in 37 versus the girls' rate of 1 in 151.

Black children with ASD often are either overlooked or misdiagnosed with other mental illnesses. A recent study showed that families and mental health practitioners are likely to mistake ASD for bad behavior. Black boys are five times more likely to be diagnosed with a conduct disorder than autism. Let that sink in: black boys with autism are more likely to be seen as morally corrupt, than autistic.

I didn't mention that to blame families and doctors who misunderstand the behaviors of autistic black children. I'm only highlighting the need for people to educate themselves on how they understand abnormal behavior in black children and to acknowledge the fact that black kids, too, can suffer from mental illnesses that affect their behavior.

Most people see a black kid misbehaving, and immediately assume he is a troublemaker, without even for a moment, considering the possibility that he may be ill. The current perception of misbehavior amongst black children must be re-examined so that they can get the help they need rather than being condemned for their symptoms.

Risk Factors

Honestly, there is no real way to protect against autism, which makes it seem as if it's the luck of the draw. And also, there is no way to predict whether someone will acquire it. All we know is that certain factors can increase the possibility of ASD.

Some of the most common risk factors for ASD are:

- **Sex:** Males are four times more likely than females to have ASD.
- **Complications during pregnancy:** Babies born before 26 weeks are at increased risk.
- **Family history:** Autism tends to run in families. People who have relatives with ASD are more likely to have it than people who don't.
- **Old Parents:** It is believed there is a connection between autism and children born to older parents.

Protective Factors

You can't prevent autism; it's a mental condition that you absolutely have no control over. However, you can lower the risk of acquiring ASD if some of the following lifestyle changes are made:

- **Live Healthily:** Have regular checkups, eat healthily, and exercise regularly. Make sure you take care of yourself during pregnancy and take the recommended vitamins and supplements.
- **Don't take drugs during pregnancy:** Ask your doctor before you take any medication, especially anti-seizure drugs.
- **Don't drink alcohol while pregnant:** Say no to that glass of wine! Avoid wine or any type of alcohol during pregnancy.

Case Example: Autism Spectrum Disorder

Tayshaun is a 17-year-old boy from New York City, currently living in a group home. He has been with foster families and group homes for most of his life. He barely remembers a time when he wasn't living in one. Before being in "the system," he lived with his grandmother, who took him in after he was removed from his mother's custody.

His mother was reported to child protective services after she was found by a neighbor lying on the floor of her apartment after overdosing on heroin. The home was a mess, the rooms were cluttered, and trash was spread all over the floors. And needles, which she used to shoot up, could be spotted in nearly every room. To make matters worse, Tayshaun, age 4 at the time, was found in a backroom wearing soiled clothes, but was surprisingly calm despite the circumstances, as if this wasn't the first time this had happened. According to child services, he had been left unattended for several hours, if not days.

Impairment from Disorder

From an early age, people noticed that something wasn't right about Tayshaun. Everyone thought he was weird. They knew he had mental issues, but no one really knew exactly what kind. He didn't respond when people called his name, almost as if he was ignoring them, which would annoy his mom and grandmother. At first, the family thought he might've had hearing issues because he seemed to be very selective in his responsiveness. He could hear like any other kid at times but would be in his own world most of the time.

Early on in school, teachers noticed Tayshaun was not fitting in well with the other students. With schoolwork, he was slightly below average compared to everyone else, but his speech and ability to make friends and play were well beneath the rest of the kids. Most of the time, Tayshaun would prefer to play alone, and would play with the same toys every day, doing the exact same things, lining them up the same way, and would have complete meltdowns if any of the other kids or a teacher would interrupt his playtime.

Most of Tayshaun's classmates avoid him because when they play with him, he is either too rough or too over-the-top with his imagination, which rarely fits into the games they're playing, and he doesn't even seem aware that he's upsetting the other children.

Also, Tayshaun's teachers noticed he wouldn't respond to questions, and when he did, he repeated the question or specific words; sometimes, he wouldn't answer at all. His attention always appeared to be on random things, like the ceiling fan spinning or playing with rubber bands or other inanimate objects as if they were toys, instead of focusing on people who attempted to talk with him. After recognizing that his social skills and communication were not as advanced as most children his age, the school staff intervened and set up an appointment for Tayshaun to see the school psychologist for psychological testing.

Mental Health Dx

Formal Diagnosis: Autism Spectrum Disorder

Justification for Diagnosis

Difficulty understanding emotions: Tayshaun does not understand he is too rough with the other children during playtime, nor does he seem aware his behavior is upsetting the other kids.

Issues with Responsiveness: Tayshaun appears to have hearing issues. Sometimes he doesn't respond when people are talking to him directly.

Speech issues: Tayshaun repeats words and phrases that don't necessarily fit into the context of the conversation, i.e., answering questions with questions or repeating certain words from a question without actually answering the question.

Odd interests: Tayshaun finds amusement with unusual objects, such as ceiling fans and rubber bands.

Rigid thinking: Tayshaun is inflexible to change. He plays with his toys in the exact same way every day and has meltdowns if anyone makes any changes.

Whew...we're finally done with the rundown of the most common mental illnesses, but I want to make a disclaimer: not everyone's mental illness is precisely the same. Some people have more symptoms than others. At the end of the day, these descriptions and case examples should be used as a guide to help you recognize the signs of a disorder if you or a loved one happens to have any symptoms.

Don't expect the symptoms to play out *exactly* like the case examples. For some, depression might present itself as a lack of motivation and not getting enough sleep. And for others, it may be sadness, guilt, and no appetite. I know that may be confusing, but if you know the basic signs of a mental illness, you should be able to recognize when someone isn't well or at least know when it's time to see a mental health professional.

Final Thoughts

"We are what we repeatedly do. Excellence, therefore, is not an act but a habit. "

–Aristotle

If you haven't realized it by now, mental health is a big deal. Our entire lives revolve around how we feel. If you aren't mentally well, chances are that other areas of your life are falling apart. I'm not saying that people with mental illnesses don't accomplish great things in life just like anyone else, because they certainly do. But it's no secret that the weight of a mental illness can create seemingly unconquerable barriers to living a satisfying life.

Wellness Takes Effort

Trying to be healthy is quite a feat if you don't know what you're doing. You can't expect to be in good shape if you don't know how to exercise or eat right. It's even more unrealistic to expect to be in good shape if you don't even attempt to take care of your health. Yet, this is the approach many of us take with our mental health. If you don't provide your mind with things that cultivate mental wellness (e.g., therapy, meditation, medication or supplements if needed) and avoid all that may be harmful (e.g., toxic people, negative self-talk, substance abuse) it is unrealistic to expect not to have mental health issues.

You wouldn't believe how many people think that a healthy mind is something that "just happens." They think you don't have to put any effort into thinking and feeling well. I will say that some of us are very fortunate to—without conscious effort—never have had a mental illness, just as some of us are lucky to have a perfect physique without working out or eating healthy. But most of us have to watch what we eat and hit the gym from time to time to keep our figure right. And mental health is no different! It would be nice if we didn't have to work on our mental health at all, but that isn't the reality for most people.

Good mental health comes from being highly intentional about it. Go out of your way to change the way you think. Remove toxic relationships from your life. Think about the things that really upset you, and ask yourself if you have really done anything to change them. If not, start today. Life is too short to *wait* for things to get better.

For far too many of us, that period of "feeling better" never comes. And not because it isn't possible, but because we do absolutely nothing to change our circumstances. James Allen, in his book *As a Man Thin-*

keth, said, "People are anxious to improve their circumstances but are unwilling to improve themselves; they, therefore, remain bound." And I couldn't agree more with this statement.

Everyone wants to be happy, yet few people will actually do the things they need to do to be happy. If you're dealing with a mental issue, whether it's big or small, it's never going to just go away. You have to take *responsibility* for the issue and do what is necessary to fix it.

Fault versus Responsibility

In life, bad things happen. If they haven't already—they will. No one makes it through this thing called life unscathed. I didn't bring this up to be negative, but to remind you that bad things will happen. You'll be fired from jobs, be cheated on, and folks will make fun of your worst insecurities. All of these things will make you feel like shit—I promise. But it's your responsibility to repair the emotional wounds that these situations cause. Yes, you read that right—it's your responsibility to resolve all adversities that come your way.

Most of the time, we confuse *fault* with responsibility. The things that happen to us aren't always our fault. It could be you were born handicapped. That, for sure, isn't your fault. Or your dad might have been a violent alcoholic that abused you as a kid. Perhaps you were poor and didn't get the same opportunities as other people you grew up with. Maybe your husband got another woman pregnant, or you had an absent parent.

I could name endless scenarios that aren't your *fault.* But guess what? It's still your responsibility to deal with the situation. Why? Because nobody else is going to swoop in and save the day. You have to be the one who finds the strength to solve your problems. It's your life, so it's your responsibility. It may not be your fault, but it's for damn sure your responsibility to figure out what you need to do to make the best of your life.

Having some "Dawg" in you can go a Long Way.

The main thing that makes humans exceptional, compared to other species, is our superior intellect. It's a blessing and a curse. Human intelligence is remarkable when you consider the wonderful feats that have been accomplished by man. Technology, medicine, and art are all due to the advanced brainpower of man. But the curse is that with great intelligence, you can be too smart for your own good, and over-think things, which leads to emotional distress. This is why, to an extent, I envy animals.

Even though animals may not be intelligent enough to build a house or drive a car like humans do, their mentality is one that humans could stand to learn from. Animals are natural go-getters that couldn't care less about how they're perceived by others. Animals know no limitations. If they want something, they go get it. They have an uncanny ability to never second guess anything, and unapologetically be themselves. They do what they want. No one else's approval is needed.

Have you ever heard the expression *he or she's got some dawg in them?* Well, if not, it's usually in reference to an individual who is unafraid of failure, and will take whatever steps necessary to succeed. This is a mentality dogs naturally have (hence the euphemism, "dawg") that many humans don't.

Dogs don't worry about insecurities. Someone can belittle a dog daily by calling it a *stupid dog*, and treat it in the most cruel and demeaning way possible. And never, I mean never, at any time will that dog start to view itself as merely a "stupid dog." A dog will never question itself based on the opinion of someone else. They simply don't have the mental capacity to internalize someone's perspective of them. Because we do have that ability, this is where we, humans, fall short.

We often adopt the negative thoughts others project onto us. Most people are like water; we flow in whatever direction we're pushed. If people tell us we're ugly, we begin to think we're ugly and start hating our natural features. If people tell us we're stupid, we stop trusting our own minds.

At some point, if you want to be happy, you have to become a *dawg*. And let what it is that you think and want for yourself be what guides your actions, not someone's unfounded opinion. At the end of the day, you're the expert on you. As a matter of fact, we're all the experts of our *own* lives and experiences, and no one can narrate our life stories better than we can.

Abandon Your Self-Image

Often our self-image is what keeps us from living the life we want to live. We let the persona that we (or others) have created stand in the way of doing what really makes us happy. That is to say, we tend to let our self-image guide us through life, rather than our real personality. Your self-image is your reputation based on the character you show to the world. Most of the time, the self-image is a fake, inhibited, self-conscious version of who you really are deep down inside. A major key to mental wellness is to abandon the self-image and embrace your true self. You have to cease to be the person you think people want you to be and be who you really are.

You're probably wondering what do I mean "be who you really are?" Well, the self-image is a shell of your real self. We create this shell to protect ourselves from rejection, judgment, and sometimes we are even rewarded for being an inauthentic shell of ourselves because it seems more appealing than our real self.

Our self-image can be helpful in many ways. It can help us make friends, get jobs, attract romantic partners, amongst many other things. But the problem with leaning on your self-image is that at some point, it always ends up backfiring, and becomes a direct contradiction of what we want — which is to be happy.

Much of the time, we paint ourselves into a corner by being too loyal to our self-image. Because of the self-image, you can no longer wear the clothes you like, you have to wear clothes that fit with the image. You can't date the person you want to date, because it's not a part of the image you've been portraying. You can't drive the car you can afford, or pursue the hobbies you're interested in—all because of this self-image. Eventually, you become so consumed by your self-image that you become disloyal to your true self, which is never good for your mental health.

Living up to a self-image always turns out badly. Why? Because it's not real. Conforming to a self-image is the ultimate form of approval seeking, which is not intended to make you happy; it's intended to shield you from rejection.

Don't do what you think will gain acceptance from other people. Self-acceptance is the only kind of acceptance you should be seeking. Do what YOU want with YOUR life, because at the end of the day, you are the one who will have to answer for the things that you did or didn't do when it's all said and done. So, if you want to be in good mental health, abandon your self-image, and seek refuge in your authentic self.

Comparison is a Thief of Joy

One thing I always say: if you want to be dissatisfied with your life, start comparing it to the lives of other people. No matter how blessed you are, if you compare your life to others, you'll eventually convince yourself of how screwed up things are for you. Trust me, you'll somehow find a way to devalue your accomplishments, and magnify your shortcomings. Comparing your life to the lives of others will always lead you down a rabbit hole of thinking you're less fortunate. That is the nature of comparison. Nothing positive ever comes from this kind of thinking. That's why it serves you no purpose.

Everyone, regardless of how perfect they seem, has flaws, setbacks, and inadequacies that they'd rather not talk about. What we don't consider when we compare is that we're only acknowledging the variables that confirm our insecurities. We needlessly compare our weaknesses and flaws to other people's strengths. And in doing so, we rob ourselves of the joys that come from our personal strengths and accomplishments.

Racehorses are known to wear small pieces of leather on each side of their heads. These garments are called "blinders." They are used to help a horse remain focused on what is in front of them during a race—the finish line. Without blinders, horses tend to get distracted by other racehorses on their left and right sides and eventually veer off the track, causing them to lose races. People have the same tendency to drift off when we pay too much attention to what others are doing. Therefore, to an extent, we have to be *blind* to what everyone else is doing and focus on our own personal finish line, whatever that might be.

Do what works

When it comes to mental health, there are no magical solutions. What works for your friends or family may not work for you, and vice versa. Some people rave about therapy, others cringe at the thought of it. Some people find medications to be helpful and couldn't imagine surviving without them; while others say, medication makes them feel like a zombie. The moral of the story is that you cannot base what works on anything but your own personal experience.

You actually have to try different things to see what works and what does not. I cannot tell you for sure what will work for you. But what I can say—without a shadow of a doubt—is that doing nothing at all is not going to help.

Ask yourself, what purpose does doing nothing serve? What do you stand to gain from doing what you've been doing? Does your current way of dealing with your problems help at all? If not, try something different. Albert Einstein said doing the same things over and over expecting different results is insanity, and I agree.

Now, not next week, not when you get a new job, not when you graduate—but now—is the right time for you to make positive changes for the better. I know that's easier said than done, but with the right amount of effort, I'm confident you can do it. And now is the perfect time.

Endnotes

1 https://www.amhca.org/blogs/joel-miller/2017/10/03/gun-violence-and-mental-illnessmyths-and-evidence-based-facts

2 https://www.helpguide.org/articles/addictions/substance-abuse-and-mental-health.htm

3 https://www.usnews.com/news/healthiest-communities/articles/2018-05-31/whats-behind-the-higher-suicide-rate-among-black-children

4 https://adaa.org/understanding-anxiety/generalized-anxiety-disorder-gad

5 https://www.ncbi.nlm.nih.gov/pmc/articles/PMC2931265/

6 https://www.nimh.nih.gov/health/statistics/major-depression.shtml

7 https://www.hhs.gov/answers/mental-health-and-substance-abuse/does-depression-increase-risk-of-suicide/index.html

8 https://namimetro.org/mental-illness/bipolar-disorder/

9 https://akfsa.org/research/prevalence-of-social-anxiety-disorder-social-phobia/

10 https://www.ncbi.nlm.nih.gov/pmc/articles/PMC4187248/

11 https://www.valleybehavioral.com/disorders/odd/signs-symptoms-causes/

12 https://www.valleybehavioral.com/disorders/odd/signs-symptoms-causes/

13 https://www.ncbi.nlm.nih.gov/pmc/articles/PMC5048197/

14 https://www.ncbi.nlm.nih.gov/pubmed/16756576

15 https://www.ncbi.nlm.nih.gov/pmc/articles/PMC4059069/

16 https://www.tandfonline.com/doi/abs/10.1080/0145935X.2011.605315?src=recsys&journalCode=wcys20

17 https://www.cambridge.org/core/journals/psychological-medicine/article/outcome-of-childhood-conduct-disorder-implications-for-defining-adult-personality-disorder-and-conduct-disorder/ABC6ACD079A7FD88D9C20F152B3E7E78

18 https://www.kennedykrieger.org/stories/linking-research-classrooms-blog/what-adhd

19 https://www.ncbi.nlm.nih.gov/pmc/articles/PMC1525089/

20 https://www.ptsd.va.gov/professional/treat/essentials/epidemiology.asp

21 https://www.ncbi.nlm.nih.gov/pmc/articles/PMC4187248/

22 https://www.mentalhelp.net/schizophrenia/statistics/

Made in the USA
Coppell, TX
14 May 2021